The Bible Speaks Today

Series Editors: J. A. Motyer (OT)
John R. W. Stott (NT)

The Message of 2 Corinthians

Power in weakness

Titles in this series

The Message of
2 Corinthians

Power in weakness

Paul Barnett
Bishop of North Sydney, Australia

Inter-Varsity Press
Leicester, England
Downers Grove, Illinois, USA

InterVarsity Press
38 De Montfort Street, Leicester LE1 7GP, England
P.O. Box 1400, Downers Grove, Illinois 60515, U.S.A.

Unless otherwise stated, quotations from the Bible are from the Holy Bible, New International Version, copyright © 1973, 1978, 1984 by the International Bible Society, New York. Used in USA by permission of Zondervan Bible Publishers, Grand Rapids, Michigan, and published in Great Britain by Hodder and Stoughton, Ltd.

Inter-Varsity Press, England, is the book-publishing division of the Universities and Colleges Christian Fellowship (formerly the Inter-Varsity Fellowship), a student movement linking Christian Unions in universities and colleges throughout the United Kingdom and the Republic of Ireland, and a member movement of the International Fellowship of Evangelical Students. For information about local and national activities in Great Britain, write to UCCF, 38 De Montfort Street, Leicester LE1 7GP.

InterVarsity Press, U.S.A., is the book-publishing division of InterVarsity Christian Fellowship, a student movement active on campus at hundreds of universities, colleges and schools of nursing. For information about local and regional activities, write Public Relations Dept., InterVarsity Christian Fellowship, 6400 Schroeder Rd., P.O. Box 7895, Madison, WI 53707–7895.

Distributed in Canada through InterVarsity Press, 860 Denison St., Unit 3, Markham, Ontario L3R 4H1, Canada.

Cover photograph: Robert Cushman Hayes

First published 1988
Reprinted 1989, 1991

Set in 11/12 pt Garamond
Typeset by Swanston Graphics Limited, Derby
Printed in England by Clays Ltd, Bungay, Suffolk

UK ISBN 0-85110-785-0 (paperback)
USA ISBN 0-8308-1228-8 (paperback)
USA ISBN 0-87784-925-0 (set of The Bible Speaks Today, paperback)

British Library Cataloguing in Publication Data

Barnett, Paul
    The message of 2 Corinthians.
    1. Bible. N.T. Corinthians, 2nd—Critical studies
    I. Title   II. Bible. N.T. Corinthians, 2nd. English. New International Version. 1984
        III. Series
    227'.306

Library of Congress Cataloging-in-Publication Data

Barnett, Paul (Paul William)
    The message of 2 Corinthians: power in weakness/Paul Barnett.
        p.   cm.—(The Bible speaks today)
    Bibliography: p.
    ISBN 0-8308-1228-8
    1. Bible. N.T. Corinthians, 2nd—Commentaries.   I. Title
    II. Title: Message of Two Corinthians.   III. Series.
BS2675.3.B28   1988
227'.307—dc19
                                        88-23382
                                        CIP

---

17   16   15   14   13   12   11   10   9   8   7   6   5   4   3
99   98   97   96   95   94   93   92   91

General preface

The Bible Speaks Today describes a series of both Old Testament and New Testament expositions, which are characterized by a threefold ideal: to expound the biblical text with accuracy, to relate it to contemporary life, and to be readable.

These books are, therefore, not 'commentaries', for the commentary seeks rather to elucidate the text than to apply it, and tends to be a work rather of reference than of literature. Nor, on the other hand, do they contain the kind of 'sermons' which attempt to be contemporary and readable, without taking Scripture seriously enough.

The contributors to this series are all united in their convictions that God still speaks through what he has spoken, and that nothing is more necessary for the life, health and growth of Christians than that they should hear what the Spirit is saying to them through his ancient – yet ever modern – Word.

J. A. MOTYER
J. R. W. STOTT
Series Editors

To Anita,
David, Peter,
Anne, Sarah

Author's preface

This is the day of the mega-commentary. Two massive studies on 2 Corinthians have recently appeared – Ralph Martin's and Victor Furnish's in the *Word* and *Anchor Bible* series, respectively. The strength of such works is their attention to detail and the exhaustive research into the meaning of the text, the cultural background of the times and the views of other commentators over the centuries. But there is a weakness inherent in these great works, despite the best efforts of the authors and their editors. It is, simply, that these commentaries are *so* large, many, many times larger than Paul's original letter. The result is that, while they are very helpful about details, they are so long that it is very difficult for the reader to stay in touch with the main themes and emphases of the apostle.

It seems to me that Paul envisaged that this letter would be read straight through, not broken up into paragraphs and studied microscopically. Of course the mega-commentaries have their place; but smaller works are also very important. One of the strengths of the *Bible Speaks Today* series is the relative brevity of the exposition it offers. The writer is able to keep the reader's attention focused on the apostle's essential message.

Among the commentaries written prior to this century, those by Calvin and Denney are still very rewarding. More recently, Barrett and Hughes have made distinguished contributions to the 2 Corinthians library – the former strongly historical, the latter powerful theologically. An outstanding brief commentary has been written by Harris.

The writing of this exposition has been a long odyssey for me. Long convinced that the letter was little read *as a whole* by

Christians, I began speaking on it at a number of Bible conferences, culminating at the Church Missionary Society Summer School at Katoomba, New South Wales, in 1977. Since then a manuscript has been prepared in several drafts until it has reached this present form. In all this, I have enjoyed the kindly patience of John Stott and of Frank Entwistle from IVP, but above all of my wife Anita and our children David, Peter, Anne and Sarah.

2 Corinthians is great biblical literature. It depicts a powerful debate between Paul on the one hand and, on the other, the alliance between his shadowy opponents who had recently come to Corinth and the local church members who supported them. It is a fascinating record of that conflict. Above all, however, the letter is important for its magnificent theological message that the power of God is brought to bear on man, not in man's power, but in his weakness. My prayer is that my exposition will allow that message to be clearly heard.

PAUL BARNETT

Contents

Chief abbreviations

AV	The Authorized (King James) Version of the Bible, 1611.
Barrett	C. K. Barrett, *The Second Epistle to the Corinthians* (A. & C. Black, 1973)
Calvin	John Calvin, *Calvin's Commentaries* (Associated Publishers and Authors, no date)
Denney	James Denney, *II Corinthians* (Hodder and Stoughton, 1894)
Eusebius	Eusebius, *The History of the Church* (AD 325; translated by G. A. Williamson, Penguin, [2]1965)
Furnish	Victor Furnish, *II Corinthians* (*Anchor Bible*, Doubleday, 1984)
Goudge	H. L. Goudge, *The Second Epistle to the Corinthians* (*Westminster Commentaries*, Methuen, 1927)
Harris	Murray Harris, *The Expositor's Bible Commentary*, vol. 10 (ed. F. Gaebelein; Zondervan, 1976)
Hughes	Philip Hughes, *Paul's Second Letter to the Corinthians* (Marshall, Morgan and Scott, 1962)
JSNT	*Journal for the Study of the New Testament*
LXX	The Old Testament in Greek according to the Septuagint, 3rd century BC
NASB	The New American Standard Bible (1963)
NIV	The New International Version of the Bible (1973, 1978, 1984)
Nov. Test.	*Novum Testamentum*
NTS	*New Testament Studies*
RSV	The Revised Standard Version of the Bible (NT 1946, [2]1971, OT 1952)
RV	The Revised Version of the Bible (NT 1881; OT 1885)
TDNT	*Theological Dictionary of the New Testament*, ed. G. W. Bromiley, 10 vols. (Eerdmans, 1964-76)

Commentary references are *ad loc.*

Introduction

1. Paul and the Corinthians

a. Paul's visits and letters to Corinth

Paul's relationships with the Corinthians span a seven-year period. In AD 50–52 he spent a year and a half in Corinth establishing the church. Some time in 55 or 56 he made a second visit (2 Cor. 13:2), what he calls a 'painful visit' (2:1), to deal with an emergency disciplinary problem in the church. In 56 or 57 he came to Corinth for the third time (13:1) and stayed for three months before taking his leave of them.[1]

Paul wrote 2 Corinthians from Macedonia in the north of Greece after his second visit to Corinth, to prepare the church for his third, final visit. Paul had decided to phase himself out of his ministry to the provinces surrounding the Aegean Sea (Asia, Macedonia, Achaia) and to establish a new work in Spain, at the western extremity of the Empire.[2] This letter and Paul's proposed farewell visit, therefore, must be seen within the apostle's wider missionary plans.

b. Differences in style between 1 and 2 Corinthians

Of the churches founded by Paul, the Corinthian church proved to be the most demanding. Their problems, both among themselves and in their relations with him, caused him to write not only the two lengthy letters we have, but also two others which have not

[1] Acts 20:3.   [2] Rom. 15:23–29.

survived – one written before, the other after, our 1 Corinthians.[3]

There are major differences of emotional tone between the two surviving letters of Paul to the Corinthians. The first indicates major problems of behaviour (*e.g.* divisions, slack moral standards, lawsuits, unkindness to the poorer or less-gifted members) and of doctrine (*e.g.* doubts about the coming resurrection of believers). There is evidence that the believers questioned Paul's abilities and authority.[4] Nevertheless the apostle writes objectively, confidently[5] and with his emotions well controlled throughout.

The second letter, however, is less well arranged than the first, and, moreover, reveals a range of emotional extremes in the author. On the one hand he is overjoyed and has confidence and pride in the Corinthians (7:4), while on the other, he is deeply hurt that they are withholding their affection from him (6:12) and that they have to 'put up' with him (11:1). Moreover, they have been ready to believe a whole range of criticisms against him – of being worldly and irresolute (1:17), of moral cowardice in writing instead of coming (1:23), of his lack of inner strength (4:16), of being demoralized and theologically deviant (4:2), of being an imposter (6:8), of being corrupt and exploitative (7:2), of not being a true minister of Christ (10:7), of being weak in speech when present and powerful only by letter, when absent (10:1, 10; 11:6, 21), of being a fool, even mad (11:1, 16, 23), of breaching convention or of craftiness in declining their financial support (11:7; 12:13–16), and of lacking mystical and miraculous credentials of ministry (12:1, 11–12). Throughout this letter Paul is forced to defend his doctrines, his ministry and his character. He expresses sorrow that the Corinthians do not reciprocate the love he had for them (6:11–13) and that they do not acknowledge the genuineness of his apostleship and what, under God, has been achieved by him among them (3:1–3; 12:11–13).

Nevertheless, despite the emotions he displays, the letter ends in a strong and confident way, evidence perhaps of Paul's God-given resilience.

c. Why were the Corinthians unhappy with Paul?

What, then, had occurred between the two letters to explain their differing characters and, in particular, to account for the battery of complaints and accusations which Paul now faced? Broadly

[3] 1 Cor. 5:9; 2 Cor. 2:3–4; 7:8–12.　　[4] 1 Cor. 2:1–5; 4:8–13.　　[5] 1 Cor. 9:2.

14

speaking, there are two factors which contributed to the Corinthians' unhappiness with the apostle, as reflected in his second letter to them.

First, there were what we might call residual cultural problems. It is evident that Paul's relationships with these southern Greeks had been strained for some time. The first letter, written about two years earlier than the second (*i.e.* in about 54 or 55) reveals that not all the Corinthians acknowledged Paul's authority as an apostle, some preferring the ministry of Apollos, others the ministry of Cephas (Peter), both of whom had visited Corinth more recently than Paul.[6] Jewish members would have been attracted to Cephas, a Palestinian Jew who had been a leading disciple among the original followers of Jesus. Educated Greek members, on the other hand, would probably have been drawn to the gifted orator Apollos, an Alexandrian Jew.[7] To the latter group, fascinated as they were by intellectualism and sophisticated discourse, Paul, the manual worker with amateurish speaking abilities, would have appeared singularly unimpressive in an age in which rhetoric and oratory were highly valued. Not least offensive to this group was Paul's utterly perverse refusal to accept money from them in patronage of his ministry, though he was not above accepting money from the rustic northerners in Macedonia (11:7–9). Moreover, his insistence on disciplinary action against wayward members still caught in (pagan) temple worship or fornication was, many of them would have felt, over-zealous. That Paul in his second letter[8] as well as in his first continued to admonish the Corinthians about idolatry and immorality indicated that these were ongoing, unresolved problems among them. It is clear that some at least of the criticisms against Paul, which are so evident in the second letter, had their origins in his earlier relationships with them.

The second and major source of criticism of Paul arose, apparently, from the recent arrival of certain Jewish 'ministers' or 'apostles' (as they called themselves; 11:13, 23), whom, however, Paul does not name or identify. These newcomers were seeking to persuade the Corinthian church that Paul's theology was in error and, specifically, that the covenant of Moses was still in force. They argued for their legitimacy as ministers on the grounds of mystic and paranormal abilities, claiming that Paul lacked these superior

---

[6] Acts 19:1; 1 Cor. 1:12; 9:5.
[7] Acts 18: 24–28.   [8] 2 Cor. 6:14 – 7:1; 12:20 – 13:1.

gifts and, moreover, that he was personally and morally deficient in many ways. The coming of these 'apostles' may have heightened some of the long-standing Corinthian criticisms of Paul as well as creating new complaints. Unquestionably the arrival of these intruding 'ministers' and their campaign against Paul's doctrines and character are the chief reason for the difference in emotional tone evident between the first and second letters.

2 Corinthians, then, was written to prepare the way for Paul's pending farewell visit to them. In it he attempts to explain why he deferred the third visit and wrote to them instead (chapters 1 – 2), expressing joy, nevertheless, that the moral problem which necessitated the second, painful visit and the (now lost) 'sorrowful' letter has been resolved (chapter 7). Further, in writing to them he urges that the collection of money for the Jerusalem church, which had lapsed, be revived and completed before his arrival (chapters 8 – 9). The major part of the letter, however, is devoted to his answer to these recently arrived 'apostles' – to their 'different gospel' (chapters 3 – 6) and to their assault on his character (chapters 10 – 13).

2. The importance of 2 Corinthians for Christian belief

Despite the structural unevenness of the letter and its emotional extremes, 2 Corinthians makes a magnificent and abiding contribution to our understanding of Christianity, in the following teachings.

a. God has proved faithful in keeping his ancient promises by his recently inaugurated *new* covenant of Christ and the Spirit (1:18–20; 3:3–6, 14–18). Moreover, God faithfully delivers and holds on to those who belong to Christ (1:3–11, 22; 4:7–9; 7:6).

b. The new covenant, based as it is on the graciousness of God (6:1), has now surpassed and replaced the old covenant (3:7–11). It powerfully meets man's needs at his points of greatest weakness — in his aging and death (4:16 – 5:10) and in his alienation from God due to sin (5:14–21).

c. Christ is the pre-existent Son of God (1:19; 8:9), the image of God (4:4), the Lord (4:5), the judge of all (5:10), the sinless one who died as substitute and representative for all people, God reconciling the world to himself through him (5:14–21). 2 Corinthians contains Paul's most comprehensive statement about the death of Christ (5:14–21).

d. Genuineness of New Testament ministry is not established by 'letters of recommendation' or by a would-be minister's mystical or miraculous powers, but by his faithfulness in persuading and his effectiveness in converting people to the Christian faith (5:11–12; 3:2–3: 10–7). The very existence of the Corinthian congregation was Christ's living letter of recommendation of Paul's ministry (3:2–3). The pattern and measure of the minister's lifestyle is the sacrifice of Christ (4:10–15; 6:1–10; 11:21–33). Establishing true criteria for genuine Christian ministry is one of the major contributions of this letter.

e. The 'word of God', the gospel, has a definable, limited content which neither ministers nor anybody else may add to or subtract from (4:2; 11:4). This gospel is exceedingly powerful in bringing rebellious humans under the rule of God (4:6; 10:4–5).

f. Paul was, both in person and through his writings, the apostle of Christ to the Gentiles. The risen Lord gave Paul this 'authority' in his historic commissioning of him on the road to Damascus (10:8; 13:10), and it is still exercised to subsequent generations through his letters, which now form part of the canon of Scripture. This letter is very important because it is Paul's major defence of his apostleship to his detractors – both ancient and modern. In it Paul answers the perennial question why he should be regarded as having authority over churches and Christians.

g. Christian giving and serving arise out of and are in response to the graciousness of God displayed towards and in us. Cheerful and generous giving, in all its forms, brings a harvest of great enrichment to the givers (chapters 8 – 9).

It is significant that Paul's expression of these teachings in this letter was inspired by the personal crisis he underwent during his rebuttal suffered on his second visit to Corinth (2:1–4, 9), his desperate escape from Ephesus (1:8–11) and his deep anxiety for the Corinthians experienced at Troas and Macedonia (2:13; 7:5–6). It is no exaggeration to say that the coming of these 'apostles' to Corinth with their 'different gospel' and their 'other Jesus', accompanied as it was by a massive assault on the integrity of Paul, could easily have spelt the end of Pauline Christianity there. That it survived and continued is probably due, in no small part, to this powerful letter.

3. Difficulties for the modern reader

Modern readers face two problems as they grapple with letters like 2 Corinthians. On the one hand we today are limited in our understanding of everyday life in a city like Corinth 2,000 years ago. With this in mind, for example, we do well to familiarize ourselves with its unique geographical position, located as it was on a narrow isthmus which was happily placed to catch the east-west sea trade and the north-south land traffic. The Roman writer Strabo described Corinth as 'always great and wealthy'. The city is estimated by some moderns at approximately 750,000 people (comparable with Adelaide or San Francisco). The interested reader is referred to the introductions to the standard scholarly commentaries for more background information about Corinth. As we read Paul's letters to these people it is worth asking ourselves: Were the Corinthians urban or rural, rich or poor, educated or uneducated, young or old, Jewish or Gentile? While our understanding of Paul's original readers must remain incomplete, much labour has been devoted to answering these and related questions. Through modern sociologically based studies, we know, for example, that the Corinthian Christians were predominately middle-class, literate city dwellers, though with numbers of poorer members as well as slaves. A few members were drawn from the upper socio-economic echelons of Achaian society. There were Jews as well as Gentiles within the congregation.[9]

The other, possibly greater, problem we face is that our only knowledge of the problems in Corinth is Paul's letter, which is written to counteract the problems as he saw them. Unfortunately he does not name or identify the 'wrongdoer', the injured party (7:12), the unnamed critic (10:7–11) or the newly arrived 'apostles' (11:13). We can only guess at the numbers and alignments of those who supported and those who opposed Paul.

The identity of the newcomers remains one of the great unsolved (and unsolvable?) mysteries of the New Testament. The data from the letter, when analysed, suggests a profile which is difficult to imagine. Clearly they are 'Hebrews ... Israelites ... Abraham's descendants' (11:22), which suggests that, like Paul,[10] they are Jews

---

[9] See also E. A. Judge, 'The Social Identity of the First Christians', *JRH* 2 (1980), pp. 201–217; R. J. Banks, *Paul's Idea of Community* (Anzea, 1979); G. Theissen, *The Social Setting of Pauline Christianity* (T. & T. Clark, 1982); W. Meeks, *The First Urban Christians* (Yale University Press, 1983).

[10] See Phil. 3:5.

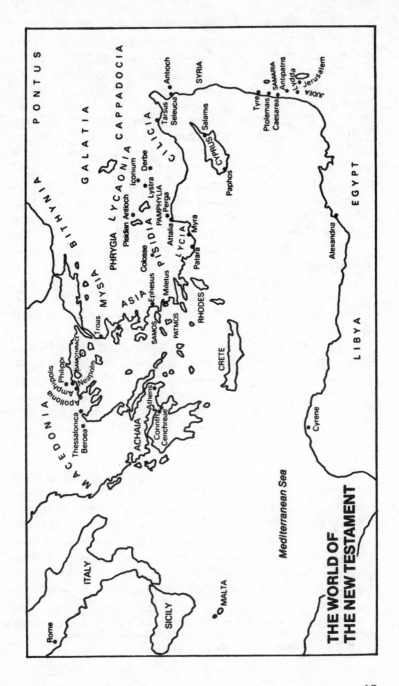

THE WORLD OF
THE NEW TESTAMENT

with roots deep within Judaism. That they are 'servants of righteousness' (11:15) suggests service of the Jewish law and of Pharisaism. Once again Paul comes to mind when he writes of himself that 'as for legalistic righteousness' he was 'faultless'.[11] His insistence that the glory of Moses is now outshone appears to be in rebuttal of the newcomers' promotion of the Mosaic covenant (3:7–17). Their missionary labours, he implied, were a (Jewish) intrusion into his (Gentile) sphere of ministry and therefore in breach of the missionary concordat at Jerusalem a decade earlier, which allocated to Paul the apostolate to the Gentiles. This side of their profile is not too difficult to comprehend, given what we know of the Judaizing, anti-Pauline mission reflected in the letter to the Galatians. Barrett's description of them as 'Jews, Jerusalem Jews, Judaizing Jews' seems accurate and appropriate.[12] Even their paranormal, ecstatic and mystic qualities (5:11–13; 12:1–6, 12) are quite capable of being located within a Jewish framework.[13]

The problem with identifying these 'ministers' lies in their ready welcome in Corinth, in particular by those who valued rhetoric and speech, the very people who were so critical of Paul for his deficiencies in this area (10:7–11). How was it possible that these 'Hebrews' were so well received by (at least some of) the educated Greek members of the Corinthian church? If these new ministers were Aramaic-speaking 'Hebrews', why does Paul need to engage in *Greek* rhetorical practices of 'comparison' and 'boasting' which are so dominant in chapters 10 – 11? The difficulty of the newcomers' identity – and this is reflected in the scholars' failure to reach a consensus – is that some of the data suggest they are Jews while other data suggest they were of Greek culture and origin.

Two comments may be made about this problem. First, it must not be assumed that being 'Hebrews ... Israelites ... Abraham's descendants', demands that they spoke only in Aramaic or Hebrew. Once again we are reminded of Paul himself, who, though a 'Hebrew born of Hebrews' and one who spoke Aramaic,[14] was also educated in the Greek language and was a competent writer of that language. It is possible that Paul's deficiencies were related to his appearance and voice, and perhaps also illness-related. Since Paul's

---

[11] Phil. 3:6.

[12] C. K. Barrett, 'Paul's Opponents in II Corinthians', *NTS* 17 (1971), pp. 233–254, for a survey of opinions on the identity of the newcomers and for Barrett's own views.

[13] P. W. Barnett, 'Opposition in Corinth', *JSNT* 22 (1984), pp. 3–17.

[14] Acts 21:40; 22:2.

written Greek reveals no small rhetorical ability,[15] it is by no means inconceivable that these Palestinian 'apostles' possessed skills of eloquence. Secondly, a close examination of the passages where Paul defends his speech (10:7–11; 11:5–6) suggests that Paul may be answering long-term, indigenous Corinthian criticisms rather than responding to comments that his rhetoric is inferior to the newcomers'. In fact the problem seems to lie with the unnamed Corinthian critic of Paul who is confident that he is Christ's minister, who complains that Paul's 'letters are weighty and forceful, but in person he is unimpressive and his speaking amounts to nothing', and who objects that Paul fails to act when present with them, being powerful only by letter from a distance (10:7–11). This person, and others with him, may have expressed this criticism of Paul for some time. The arrival of the newcomers, with their mystical gifts, may have provoked further opposition of Paul from sections of the Corinthian church who were already critical of him.

Paul writes of 'super-apostles' (11:5; 12:11) and 'false apostles ... masquerading as apostles of Christ' (11:13). Are these one and the same or are they different? While many suggest that the 'super-apostles' were *the* apostles, leaders of the Jerusalem church like James and Peter, this seems unlikely. The context identifies the 'super-apostles' (11:5) as those who have come to Corinth proclaiming 'another Jesus' and 'a different gospel'. In 1 Corinthians 15:11 Paul is emphatic that he and the apostles proclaim the *same* gospel. It seems better to say that the 'super-apostles' were, in fact, the 'false apostles'.[16]

What, then, was the mission of these newcomers in Corinth? These 'apostles' do not appear to be promoting the circumcision of the Gentiles, as the Judaizers had done ten years earlier, reflected in Galatians. 2 Corinthians does not refer to the Gentile-circumcision dispute. As I have suggested elsewhere, theirs may have been a two-pronged mission, directed on the one hand to Jews and on the other to Gentiles.[17] The complaint made against Paul in Jerusalem was that he told Jews to abandon Moses, the circumcising of their children and the Jewish customs, and that he did not impose the Jerusalem decree requiring Gentiles to desist from idol-sacrificed meat and eat only kosher-butchered meat.[18] Quite possibly these

---

[15] See, *e.g.*, the poetic thirteenth chapter of 1 Corinthians.
[16] See P. W. Barnett, *op.cit.*   [17] *Ibid.*
[18] Acts 21:20–25.

carefully phrased criticisms of Paul in Jerusalem represented the main elements of the Judaizing anti-Pauline agenda. On this theory these 'apostles' sought to maintain Jewish Christians in Corinth within the Mosaic covenant and to bring Gentile Christians under the requirements of the Jerusalem decree. These are some of the difficulties for the modern reader. Nevertheless, despite such gaps in our knowledge, the message of the greater part of the letter is clear enough.

I Explanations: why Paul wrote instead of coming (1:1 – 2:13)

1:1–11
1. God and Paul

Events of deep distress to Paul form the immediate background to the second letter to the Corinthians. Corinth and Ephesus, centres to which important missionary labour had been devoted, had become focal points of profound personal difficulty for him. At Corinth he, their father in the faith, had been rebuffed and criticized. In Ephesus a city-wide riot had occurred over his ministry so that it was no longer safe to remain there. Unwelcome in the one and endangered in the other, he went to Macedonia where he began to write his letter. First he greeted his readers and praised God for comforting him in his recent sufferings. Then he proceeded to tell them what had happened since his 'painful' visit to Corinth and to explain why he was writing instead of returning immediately. As in his other letters Paul introduced near the beginning what would be a major theme throughout, in this case his experience of suffering.

1. The apostle to the church (1:1a)

Paul, an apostle of Christ Jesus by the will of God, and Timothy our brother ...

By his opening words, *Paul, an apostle ... by the will of God,*[1] Paul pointedly reminds the Corinthians, some of whom were questioning his authority, that he is not an apostle by self-appointment but *by the will of God*. From their point of view he had been but one of a number of notable ministers who had visited Corinth. Apollos and Cephas (= Peter), perhaps in their own ways more impressive than

---

[1] In placing his name and title at the *beginning* of the letter, Paul was following the convention of that time. The word *apostle* meant someone sent by, and acting as an agent for, someone else; a delegated representative.

23

Paul, had been in Corinth more recently and had created, no doubt unintentionally, their own factions within the church.[2] Even more recently a group of ministers had arrived whom Paul neither names nor identifies, but who had actively opposed his teaching and influence among the Corinthians.[3] Understandably some of the Corinthians were wondering why Paul thought his relationship with them was special.

For his part Paul based his claim to be an apostle on the Damascus Road event when the risen Christ appeared and instructed him: 'I will send (*apostellō*) you ... to the Gentiles.'[4] Fundamental to Paul's ministry, therefore, was the 'revelation' (*apokalypsis*) of God, received near Damascus, that Jesus the Son of God had commissioned him to evangelize the Gentiles.[5] Paul's complete loyalty to Christian ministry over many years, even though he had been a leading persecutor of the church, led the 'pillar' apostles James, Cephas and John, at a meeting in Jerusalem, to recognize, formally, that Paul 'had been entrusted (*i.e.* by God) with the gospel to the uncircumcised ... an apostolate (*apostolē*) to the Gentiles'.[6] Paul's sphere of ministry among the Gentiles, and therefore among the Corinthians, was assigned to him by God (10:13). His right to exercise a ministry among them, both by letter and by physical presence, was not based on empty demand but arose out of the 'authority the Lord gave us for building ... up' the Corinthians (10:8; 13:10). Paul, therefore, was *an apostle ... by the will of God*, as he often stated.[7]

At the beginning of the letter Paul is establishing his apostleship as a point of contrast with these newly arrived ministers who, apparently, also presented themselves as 'apostles' (11:13). They based their claim on 'letters of recommendation' (3:1) as demonstrated by supposedly 'superior' displays of gifts, superior, that is, to Paul's gifts (11:5–6; 12:11–12). Paul described them as 'false apostles (*pseudapostoloi*) masquerading as apostles of Christ' (11:13). The opening words of this letter indicate Paul's concern to impress upon the Corinthians his credentials as a genuine apostle of Christ. It is striking that while the *basis* of Paul's apostleship was Christ's Damascus Road call, the *evidence* he gives in support relates to his

---

[2] Acts 18:24 – 19:1; 1 Cor. 1:12; 3:5; 9:5; 16:12.
[3] 2 Cor. 2:17 – 3:1; 10:12; 11:4–5, 12–14, 20–23.
[4] Acts 22:21; 26:17; 9:15.
[5] Gal. 1:12, 16.   [6] Gal. 2:7–8, my translation.
[7] Eph. 1:1; Col. 1:1; *cf.* Gal. 1:1.

24

lifestyle – a lifestyle characterized by the sacrifice of Christ expressed in apostolic ministry. Although he could point to the existence of the Corinthian church as a 'letter of recommendation' and refer minimally to mystical and miraculous elements in his ministry,[8] his chief self-characterization was in a life of hardship, conflict and weakness as the bearer of the word of God focused on the death and resurrection of Jesus. While the source of Paul's authority was Christ, his authority was attested not by marvels or mysteries but, as Barrett helpfully puts it, 'in the pattern of death and resurrection stamped upon his own life and work'. Sacrifice and self-giving were for Paul, as they remain for us, indispensable evidence of genuineness as Christian believers.

This letter also comes from Paul's colleague Timothy who is, by contrast, referred to as *our* (lit. 'the') *brother*, or fellow Christian. This should remind us that, although Timothy was a missionary and a Christian leader, he was not an apostle of Christ. Although there may be no harm in using the word 'apostle' metaphorically of certain Christian leaders today, it is unhelpful to use the word in a theological sense apart from those to whom it is applied in the New Testament. Some ministers today, like Paul's opponents in Corinth, also call themselves 'apostles' to reinforce their authority over churches. It is preferable to limit the use of the word 'apostle' to *the* apostles within the apostolic age.

2. The church of God (1:1b)

To the church of God at Corinth, together with all the saints throughout Achaia.

What would the Corinthians have understood Paul to mean when he addressed them as *the church*? For many today the word means either a religious building or Christianity as an institution. Paul's readers, however, would have understood *church (ekklēsia)* as an everyday term for a gathering of people or, more technically, for an official assembly such as a parliament or court. Both meanings can be illustrated from Acts 19, where on the one hand there is reference to an 'assembly' of the people of Ephesus (verse 41), and on the other to the 'legal assembly' of the city council (verse 39). Clearly the Corinthians would have read Paul's words as being directed to the 'gathering' or 'assembly' of Christians in Corinth.

[8] 2 Cor. 3:2; 5:13; 12:1–6; 12:12.

But what did Paul mean? The word *ekklēsia* occurred frequently in the Greek Old Testament, the Septuagint,[9] which Paul usually quoted. There it was used of great 'gatherings' of the people of God, for example when 'all the tribes of Israel stood before the Lord in the assembly (*ekklēsia*) of the people of God'.[10] As the people of Israel met, it was in the awareness that they 'stood before the Lord'. Similarly, King David addressed Solomon with the words: 'I charge you before the whole assembly (*ekklēsia*) of the Lord, and in the audience of our God.'[11] In the New Testament Stephen spoke of God's gathered people as 'the congregation (*ekklēsia*) in the desert' for whose sake Moses received 'living words' from the angel of God.[12] In addressing them as 'the church of God' Paul meant the Corinthian believers to understand that in their gathering together they were all that the gathered tribes of Israel had been – the church of God, no less. If to us *church* means a religious building or institution and to the Corinthians it simply meant an assembly of any kind, to Paul it meant specifically 'an assembly' of God's people in God's presence to hear God's word.

It may be observed that the substance of this letter is encapsulated within the first verse: 'the apostle ... to the church'. Here on the one hand is the church; here on the other is the apostle who now addresses it. The question is: Will the church at Corinth submit to the authority of the apostle Paul? There is no doubt that Paul claimed such authority,[13] and it seems that the Corinthians ultimately followed Paul, not the intruding ministers. The very survival of his letters is evidence of that.

The question for the next generation of Corinthian Christians, and indeed for us today, is: Are Paul's letters authoritative outside the immediate period in which he lived and wrote? Are they 'Scripture' for us? Was he right in claiming this authority?

Let me suggest two reasons for accepting Paul's authority today. First, he did not write his letters merely for the immediate circumstances of the addressees. He directed that his letters were to be read in churches other than those to whom they were addressed.[14] The formal and weighty nature of Paul's letters suggests that he expected them to benefit readers beyond the immediate recipient group. Secondly, Paul's Christ-given authority over the Gentiles

---

[9] So called because of the belief that seventy people had been involved in the translation three centuries earlier.

[10] Ju. 20:2, LXX.   [11] 1 Chr. 23:8, LXX.   [12] Acts 7:38.

[13] 2 Cor. 10:8–11; 13:10; *cf.* 1 Cor. 14:36–38.   [14] Col. 4:16.

existed as much in physical absence through his letters as in physical presence through his preaching.[15] There can be no doubt that the original apostles regarded Paul as an apostle and his writings as Scripture.[16] From post-apostolic times his letters were recognized in the churches as part of the canon of Scripture, alongside the four gospels and the Old Testament. While in these distant times his intention is not always clear to us, we are no more free now than the Corinthians were then to behave and do as we choose. The writings of Paul, then, declare a gospel to be believed and yield principles of behaviour to be followed in both the first and the twentieth century.

In addressing his readers as *saints* Paul does not imply that they were exceptionally heroic or devout, as we infer from the word, but rather that they were, in God's eyes, his 'holy people'.[17] The Bible speaks of 'saints' as quite ordinary people whom God graciously regards as special to him through their faith-commitment to his Son Jesus. Moreover, God not only treats believers as holy, he actively makes them so by the dynamic presence of the Holy Spirit in the inner recesses of their lives, conforming them to the pattern of Christ.[18]

In addition to the gathered congregation in Corinth, the capital, the letter-writer also greets readers *throughout* (the province of) *Achaia*. While the narrative of the Acts[19] and the two letters provide considerable data about Christianity in Corinth, knowledge of Christians in the wider province is limited to a few brief references.[20] Certainly the Corinthians in themselves were unworthy to be regarded as the *church of God* or as *saints* or 'holy ones'. We have only to consider their unloving and even immoral behaviour set out in the first letter.[21] Even more seriously, this present letter shows them to be interested in the 'other' Jesus as presented by the false apostles (11:3–4). Despite this Paul does not disown them as Christians or repudiate their profession of church membership.

Subsequent Christians have not always been as charitable as Paul. There have been many instances where differences over tiny or obscure points of theology have led to bitter division, with one group unchurching the other, in the name of doctrinal purity. The

[15] 2 Cor. 10:8–13; cf. Phil. 2:12.   [16] Gal. 2:7–9; 2 Pet. 3:16.
[17] The words 'holy' and 'saint' are the same in Greek (*hagios*).
[18] 2 Cor. 3:18; Rom. 12:1–2.
[19] Acts 18:1–18, 27 – 19:1.   [20] Athens (Acts 17:34), Cenchreae (Rom. 16:1–2).
[21] 1 Cor. 1:11–12 (divisions), 5:1–2 (toleration of ?incest), 6:1 (lawsuits), 8:9 (uncaring behaviour to weak Christians), 11:17–21 (uncaring behaviour to the poor), 13:1–3 (egocentric, unloving, display of gifts).

church in Corinth fell far short of the standards of belief and behaviour many since that time have demanded. Nevertheless Paul addresses the Corinthians as *the church of God*, as God's 'holy ones', and teaches and exhorts them to behave as if they were.

3. Paul's prayer (1:2)

Grace and peace to you from God our Father and the Lord Jesus Christ.

It was a convention in ancient letters for the writer to express pious wishes for the health and well-being of his readers, invoking the names of the gods. Although he observed this practice in the form of his greeting, the apostle introduced the distinctively Christian hope that his readers will enjoy *grace and peace* which come *from God our Father and the Lord Jesus Christ*. Nevertheless, the words used here by Paul do not have any special force in this letter, since they are found in identical form in greetings in six other letters.[22] In brief, the peace for which Paul prays is that blessed enjoyment of harmonious fellowship with God our Father enjoyed by those who have taken hold of his *grace* or graciousness shown them in the birth and death of *the Lord Jesus Christ* (8:9; 6:1).

4. Blessed be God (1:3–7)

Praise be to the God and Father of our Lord Jesus Christ, the Father of compassion and the God of all comfort, [4]who comforts us in all our troubles, so that we can comfort those in any trouble with the comfort we ourselves have received from God. [5]For just as the sufferings of Christ flow over into our lives, so also through Christ our comfort overflows. [6]If we are distressed, it is for your comfort and salvation; if we are comforted, it is for your comfort, which produces in you patient endurance of the same sufferings we suffer. [7]And our hope for you is firm, because we know that just as you share in our sufferings, so also you share in our comfort.

If in his opening sentences Paul follows the established letter-writing format, in the next five sentences he observes another convention, also christianized, the Jewish blessing of God. Those who attended the synagogue of that time would pray, 'Blessed art thou, O Lord our God and God of our fathers.'[23] The re-shaping of this prayer, now directed to 'the God and Father of our Lord Jesus

[22] Rom. 1:7; 1 Cor. 1:3; Gal. 1:3; Eph. 1:2; Phil. 1:2 and Phm. 3 have the identical phrase in the Greek.
[23] The First Benediction, quoted in Barrett, p. 58.

Christ', gives some indication of the impact of Jesus as the Son of God on early Jewish Christian believers like Paul and Peter.[24] The christianization of both the greeting and blessing as expressions, respectively, of Greek culture and Jewish religion, are evidence for the profound conversion to Christianity of the Hellenistic Jew, Saul of Tarsus. As with so much else in this letter, what he writes here is a direct commentary on his own personal circumstances. In the midst of acute suffering (1:8–9) Paul had experienced the comfort of God, and for this he devoutly declared his blessing on *the Father of compassion and the God of all comfort* (verse 3). He was also locked in a fierce debate with the Judaizing 'apostles' who proclaimed what Paul calls 'another Jesus'.[25] It was important for him to establish at the outset that God, the God of the Old Testament and of the Jews, was *the Father of our Lord Jesus Christ* (verse 3). God is to us the Father of Jesus and also '*our*' Father' (verse 2). Let those Corinthians who were succumbing to the Judaizing influence understand that God is able to be known as *Father* only as they acknowledge Jesus to be God's Son and their *Lord*. Their understanding of Jesus' relationship with God profoundly affected their own relationship with God. To reject Jesus as Lord would be to repudiate God as Father.

Paul's blessing of God is tightly packed with interlocking ideas, three of which we now examine.

a. Christ's sufferings carry over to us

In writing *the sufferings of Christ flow over into our lives* (verse 5), Paul is teaching that some kind of solidarity exists between Christ and his people. Jesus foresaw that both he and his followers would suffer. God would 'strike the shepherd,' he said, 'and the sheep will be scattered.'[26] He was referring not only to the events of the evening of his arrest but also to the scattering of his followers throughout the whole period until his return. Moreover, he taught that he and his followers were one in ministry both received and withheld. Referring to the future withholding of food, clothing and care from his 'brothers' the disciples, he said, 'Whatever you did not do for one of the least of these, you did not do for *me*.'[27] Paul had good reason to understand this. After Paul had heaped suffering on the

[24] Eph. 1:3; 1 Pet. 1:3.   [25] 2 Cor. 11:4–6, RSV.
[26] Mark 14:27, but see Zc. 13:7–9.
[27] Mt. 25:45. See T. W. Manson, *The Sayings of Jesus* (SCM, London, 1961), pp. 248–252.

29

believers, the risen Lord asked him, 'Saul, Saul, why do you persecute *me*?'[28] This understanding of the solidarity of Christians with Christ in his suffering is by no means confined to Paul. Peter told his readers in Asia Minor to 'rejoice ... as you participate in the sufferings of Christ'.[29] The messianic age began with the coming of Jesus; but it is an age marked by sufferings – his own and those of his people.

In this short paragraph the verbs and nouns for *comfort* (which presupposes suffering) occur ten times, for *trouble* three times and for *suffer(ing)* four times'. Directly or indirectly, suffering is referred to seventeen times in five verses! But to which suffering is he referring? Paul had in mind, in particular, what he called *troubles* (verse 4). The Greek word contains the idea of 'pressure', the 'pressure' which he felt as a result of his ministry. Paul's challenge to idols and idolatry in Ephesus brought upon him such an oppressive sense of burden that he expected to die as a result of the experience (1:8–9). His insistence on sincere repentance among the Corinthians led him to write to them 'out of great distress and anguish of heart and with many tears' (2:4; *cf.* 7:8–10). While Paul doubtless was as prone to money worries, health problems and relationship conflicts as other people, faithfulness to Christ and to the ministry were the chief source of his *troubles*.

b. God comforts us

God is *the Father of compassion* (verse 3), which means he is a compassionate Father as well as the source of all compassion. Moreover, he is *the God of all comfort* (verse 3) something which reminds us of God's call to Isaiah to 'comfort, comfort my people' (Is. 40:1). That this may be a picture of motherly tenderness is implied by God's words through Isaiah: 'As a mother comforts her child, so will I comfort you' (Is. 66:13). The God of the Greeks, by contrast, was quite indifferent to human pain. This deity, which merely existed, possessed no knowable qualities and exerted no influence in the world. The God who is revealed in the Bible, however, has knowable qualities (*the God of all comfort*) and is active in his creation (he *comforts us*).

If God is the source of mercy and comfort, Christ is the channel through whom these things come to us. It is *through Christ* that *our*

[28] Acts 9:4.   [29] 1 Pet. 4:13.

comfort overflows (verse 5). This means, as in all our relationships with God, we seek *comfort* and *compassion* in the name of Jesus, that is, as Christian believers. Whatever doctrines about Jesus the newcomers were teaching, the apostle made it clear that while all good things have their origin in God, they come to us through Christ. Thus he taught that not only the 'new creation' and 'reconciliation' (5:18) but also 'comfort' and 'compassion' come to us from God, through Christ

c. We are to comfort others

These verses teach us that Christian believers are united both with Christ and with one another. On the one hand, both troubles and comfort come to us through Christ; on the other, *we can comfort those in any trouble with the comfort we ourselves have received from God* (verse 4). The comfort we receive from God through Christ we are both to give to and receive from one another. God's comfort, therefore, is not to terminate on the one who receives it. God comforted Paul by the coming of Titus to Macedonia (7:6), just as Titus had previously been comforted by the Corinthians (7:7). Paul in turn will comfort the Corinthians (verse 6), God's comfort thus having come full circle, from the Corinthians, through Titus to Paul, back to the Corinthians.

The intimacy of relationships in and between the New Testament churches is striking. Because the members knew one another they were able to give and receive comfort. In modern churches we often shrink from those relationships through which the comfort of God could be imparted. How are we to comfort others? Clearly we need to care about others and to be sensitive to their feelings and emotions, to 'rejoice with those who rejoice; mourn with those who mourn'.[30] Modern counselling methods stress the importance of paying serious attention, with full eye-contact, as people speak to us. There is, moreover, a helpful emphasis on identifying the emotions, including depression. If we would be used by God to comfort and encourage, we must be prepared to listen without interruption so as to allow others to express to us their deepest feelings. While all Christian ministry must be directed ultimately to the mind and the will, it will frequently begin with the emotions.

[30] Rom. 12:15.

Power and weakness, which together represent the unifying theme of this letter, are hinted at in this opening paragraph. All believers, like Paul and the Corinthians, suffer the weakness of *troubles* through their Christian service. Nevertheless the power of God in his mercies and *comfort* meets us at our point of need. Great though our sense of weakness may be, the power of God is always greater. Some ministers today unhelpfully raise the hopes of their people by promising them immediate health and prosperity, as their due portion from God. These promises appear to be tailor-made for a society whose need for instant gratification is unprecedented in history. Paul, by contrast, soberly refers to his readers' *sufferings*, and he promises, not immediate healing and success, but God's *comfort* which they will experience as they patiently endure (verse 6).

5.   God is a deliverer (1:8–11)

We do not want you to be uninformed, brothers, about the hardships we suffered in the province of Asia. We were under great pressure, far beyond our ability to endure, so that we despaired even of life. [9]Indeed, in our hearts we felt the sentence of death. But this happened that we might not rely on ourselves but on God, who raises the dead. [10]He has delivered us from such a deadly peril, and he will deliver us. On him we have set our hope that he will continue to deliver us, [11]as you help us by your prayers. Then many will give thanks on our behalf for the gracious favour granted us in answer to the prayers of many.

The 'sufferings' and 'troubles' of the previous paragraph are now to be expanded upon. He relates to the Corinthians the terrible ordeal he had experienced back in Ephesus and explains how God had delivered him.

a.   Hardships in Asia

Paul calls what occurred in Ephesus *the hardships we suffered in ... Asia*, something he amplifies further as having been *under great pressure, far beyond our ability to endure* (verse 8). Here the picture is of a ship being weighed down as by the ballast, or of being 'crushed' (RSV). Those who have experienced or are familiar with depression will feel that Paul's imagery has a modern psychological ring to it. Two qualifying phrases add to the severity of the description. The first, *great* (Greek, *kath' hyperbolēn*) means, by implication, 'that which exceeds' or 'surpasses' description. The second, *far beyond our ability to endure* (Greek, *hyper dynamin*) is literally 'beyond (our) power'. The whole phrase could be paraphrased as: 'We were indescribably, beyond the limits of our power, brought down into the depths.'

We have discussed this phrase in detail for two reasons. First, Paul's words describe his state of mind at the time of writing so graphically that they warrant a more extensive treatment. Secondly, Paul will use the three key ideas ('power', 'weight', 'indescribable') in important later passages, where, however, he will turn them upside down so as to indicate the surpassing 'power' of God, the 'indescribable' glory, and the 'power' of Christ perfected in weakness.[31]

Naturally we would like to know precisely what had happened to Paul in Asia for him to write *we despaired even of life* (verse 8), and *we felt the sentence of death* (verse 9). The verb *felt* (RSV 'received') translates the Greek perfect tense, suggesting that the death sentence had already been passed but was not yet executed. Various 'death sentences' have been suggested; for example, serious illness, an Ephesian imprisonment, and the riot in Ephesus.[32] The latter appears the most likely. Was it the case that the silversmiths' conspiracy made Paul realize that his ministry would always bring him into conflict with those whose livelihood depended on the religious beliefs his gospel committed him to reject? Moreover, wherever he went, the Jews conspired against him,[33] so that later in the letter he wrote both of 'danger from my own countrymen' (*i.e.* Jews) and 'danger from Gentiles' (11:26). Our suggestion, and it must remain a suggestion, is that from the experience in Asia, he knew it was only a matter of time before the various forces pitted against him would succeed. By the goodness of God, however, Paul had received a reprieve: God *delivered us from such a deadly peril* (verse 10).

b. Deliverance

If Paul had received *the sentence of death* he had also come to *rely on God* (verse 9) and to set his *hope* on God (verse 10). The Greek verbs are in the perfect tense, indicating events in the past with continu-

---

[31] 2 Cor. 4:7 (*hyperbolē ... dynameos*); 4:17 (*kath' hyperbolēn eis hyperbolēn aiōnion baros doxēs*); 12:9 (*dynamis en astheneia teleitai*).

[32] Acts 19:23–34.

[33] *E.g.* Acts 20:3, 19.

33

ing consequences. Thus the ordeal in Asia, whatever it was, still impinged on Paul while also stimulating ongoing reliance and hope in God. We may say that the new, deep awareness of death was accompanied by a new, deep trust in God.

Through the experience of utter helplessness Paul had come to a new appreciation of the power of the God *who raises the dead* (verse 9), referring, that is, to God's recent deliverance of Paul. The God on whom Paul relied was the living God, the God who continues to act now. He was not only the God who 'raised the Lord Jesus' (past tense) and who 'will ... raise us' (future tense) (4:14; 5:15), he is also the God who continues to raise the dead (present tense), that is, metaphorically, to deliver his people from dire circumstances (verse 9). It is good that the great saving acts of God in the historic resurrection of Jesus and the coming resurrection of believers have been set in the creeds of the church. It is, however, very easy to regard this God as remote and distant from our present situation, to think of him as the God of theology and not of reality. Ministers-in-training need to be taught about the God of yesterday and the God of tomorrow. But if they lack personal confidence in the God of today, how will they help their people in the manifold crises of life? In the same way, practising pastors must not shrink from the problems encountered by their people. Rather, they must draw their people into a deeper confidence in God who will comfort and sustain them. In writing that the experience in Asia was to make him *rely ... on God* (verse 9), Paul shows us that God's power reached even into those evil circumstances to draw Paul into a deeper relationship with himself.

Paul's confidence that God *has delivered us* and that *he will deliver us* again (verse 10) refers both to God's ultimate deliverance in the great resurrection and also to God's interim deliverance from day-to-day problems. Paul did not separate the God of the creeds from the God on whom he depended each day. Intellectually inclined Christians tend to emphasize the former, and experience-oriented Christians the latter; but for Paul there was no contradiction. The interim deliverance has caused Paul to trust God more deeply for the final deliverance when he will raise his people from the dead.

We should remember, however, that God's 'deliverances' in this life are always partial. We may recover from an illness, but there is no way to sidestep our last enemy, death. We are inextricably tangled in the sorrow and suffering of the world, whose form is passing away.[34] Only in the resurrection of the dead is there perfect deliverance.

c. Prayer

It is no accident that the references to God's deliverance of Paul and to prayer are placed side by side. The God who *raises the dead* (verse 9) and who *delivered* Paul *from such a deadly peril* is responsive to prayer. As the Corinthians are united in prayer for Paul they are said to be *helping* or 'working together' with God (verse 11), though there is no suggestion that God is dependent upon human help or prayers.[35] Nevertheless, Paul envisaged that *by your prayers* the blessing of deliverance from peril would be *granted* so that *many* would *give thanks* to God. Although he had now come to Macedonia he still faced danger. The Corinthians were powerless to help, being hundreds of miles away, yet Paul was confident that God, through their united prayers, would do what they in themselves could not do – deliver Paul from trouble. The words *in answer to the prayers of many* stand in the original, literally, as 'out of many faces',[36] which may perhaps be understood as the beautiful picture of many faces upturned to God in thanksgiving.

This brief sentence refers both to *prayer* and to giving *thanks*, indicating the important and close connection between them. Prayer to God for specific needs is rightly followed by thanksgiving; indeed the one is incomplete without the other. According to Furnish, 'petition no less than thanksgiving is rooted in a profound trust in the power and goodness of God'.

Modern man is so blinded by his technology and his own sense of power that he regards prayer and thanksgiving as weak, useless and a joke. The reality, however, is that everybody is at the mercy of social, political and economic forces. The apprehension that human omnipotence is in fact an illusion is a precondition to the discovery, or rediscovery, of the power of God and of prayer and thanksgiving. Paul's helplessness in the face of strong forces led him to experience, doubtless through prayer, the power of God to deliver him.

---

[34] 1 Cor. 7:31.

[35] Unlike the views of the Pharisees as expounded by Paul's later contemporary the Jewish historian Josephus. According to him, Pharisees taught that human free will is the major factor in action, God merely co-operating with human decision. See *The Jewish War* ii, 162–163.   [36] Alternatively, 'from many people'.

1:12–22
2. Reply to Corinthian criticism

In popular novels nothing ever goes wrong for the hero. He strides through each episode of the story with success after success. It is not like that for ordinary people in real life; it was not like that for Paul. Because he did not return immediately to Corinth, as he had indicated he would, the Corinthians now regard Paul as a double-minded man, unable to stick to his plans. One senses in these words of Paul that nothing he can say will be able to change the Corinthians' opinion about him. And yet from his viewpoint he had the best of reasons for changing his plans and honourable motives for doing so.

1. The Corinthian criticism (1:12–17)

Now this is our boast: Our conscience testifies that we have conducted ourselves in the world, and especially in our relations with you, in the holiness and sincerity that are from God. We have done so not according to worldly wisdom but according to God's grace. [13]*For we do not write to you anything you cannot read or understand And I hope that,* [14]*as you have understood us in part, you will come to understand fully that you can boast of us just as we will boast of you in the day of the Lord Jesus.*

[15]*Because I was confident of this, I planned to visit you first so that you might benefit twice.* [16]*I planned to visit you on my way to Macedonia and to come back to you from Macedonia, and then to have you send me on my way to Judea.* [17]*When I planned this, did I do it lightly? Or do I make my plans in a worldly manner so that in the same breath I say, 'Yes, yes' and 'No, no'?*

The defensive nature of his words reveals that Paul was under strong criticism from the Corinthian church, or a section of it. They felt that he had *conducted* himself badly both *in the world* and also in his *relations with* them (verse 12). Specifically in question were his *sincerity* and *wisdom* (verse 12), and they alleged that what he had written to them was difficult to *understand* (verse 13). No less serious was their belief that Paul was a vacillating, *worldly* man ready to say Yes and No *in the same breath* (verse 17).

What had Paul done to provoke this hostility in Corinth? Their complaints arose from the changes Paul had made to his plans to come and see them before he finally withdrew from the Aegean region. Originally,[1] when the churches of Corinth and Ephesus were relatively stable, he had written that his withdrawal plan would be Asia → Macedonia → Achaia → Judea. But after writing 1 Corinthians it was necessary to make an unscheduled 'painful' visit (2:1) to Corinth during which he said that he would return to them before going to Macedonia (verses 15–16). However, instead of coming back to them immediately, he wrote a letter (1:23; 2:4), and reverted to his original plan to go first to Macedonia and then to Achaia. Looking at things from the Corinthians' standpoint, Paul had made major changes to his plans and could be seen to be a vacillating man whose behaviour reflected a *worldly* rather than a godly wisdom. But is this fair to Paul?

While there is no claim that the apostles were other than sinful, fallible humans, there were a number of factors about Paul's circumstances which explain and justify his behaviour. First, it became apparent by the time he left Corinth that the problem which occasioned his visit was still unresolved. If one visit failed, would another, hard on the heels of the first, achieve anything further? Back in Ephesus he may well have reasoned that a letter and time for the Corinthians to think things over might be a better approach. As it happened the (lost) letter to the Corinthians did bring about a resolution to the problem (7:5–16). Secondly, a crisis had occurred in Ephesus which put his life at risk and which necessitated his withdrawal (1:9).[2]

Although Paul refrains from saying so, it may have been the Corinthians who were in the wrong in this matter. Instead of showing loving concern for him in his grave difficulties in Ephesus they had written him off as unspiritual and vacillating. We do well to avoid such ill-formed and unkind opinions as shown by the Corinthians. Let the facts first be gathered and explanations provided before firm opinions are reached. Then, if something bad

[1] Acts 19:21; 1 Cor. 16:5–7.   [2] Acts 20:1.

has occurred, let our response be tempered with the meekness and gentleness which Paul said was the mark of his ministry (10:1). These considerations are advanced to explain Paul's actions. But what does he say?

2. Paul's response

Paul's reply, when reduced to basics, is that he has interrogated his *conscience* (verse 12) in prospect of *the day of the Lord Jesus* (verse 14), when, as he states elsewhere, 'the Lord ... will expose the motives of men's hearts'.[3] The testimony of his conscience is that, on that day, Paul will be shown to have behaved both in the world at large and towards the Corinthians with holiness and *sincerity that are from God* (verse 12). These motives have been operative, his conscience tells him, both in the former (lost) letter as well as in the present one. He had written so as to be understood, which *in part* he was; he now writes with the intention that the Corinthians *will understand fully* (verse 14). Their questioning of his motives is ill based. When the great and coming day arrives and everything is revealed he is confident that they will be *boast* of him.

The word *boast*, which is common in this letter,[4] has an ugly and un-Christian ring to it. It must be remembered, however, that boasting of achievement was common among both Gentiles and Jews. As a matter of convention successful Roman soldiers commemorated their victories in wall paintings and in epic narratives. Jesus' parable of the Pharisee in the temple tells us of the man's confidence in his religious deeds.[5] Paul's opponents, the visitors in Corinth, appear to have boasted of their credentials and experiences to legitimize their mission; they 'are boasting in the way the world does', he writes (11:18). In using their style, but boasting rather of 'weakness', (12:9), of the 'Lord' (10:17), and, in this case, in *God's grace* (verse 12), Paul is actually inverting their practice and throwing it back in their teeth. So far from revealing arrogance, which indeed it does in his critics, Paul's boasting actually reflects his humility before the Lord. In particular the apostle is concerned to show that his motives, irreproachable as they are, do not arise from within himself, from *worldly wisdom*, but from *God's grace*. Barrett comments that 'out of the theology of the grace of God emerge, as gifts from God himself, the ethical virtues of *simplicity*

---

[3] 1 Cor. 4:5.   [4] Noun and verb forms occur twenty-five times.   [5] Lk. 18:12.

and *sincerity*. This is the foundation of Paul's argument in this paragraph; and it ought to be recognized by the Corinthians themselves.'

3. God is faithful to his promises (1:18–20)

But as surely as God is faithful, our message to you is not 'Yes' and 'No'. [19]For the Son of God, Jesus Christ, who was preached among you by me and Silas and Timothy, was not 'Yes' and 'No', but in him it has always been 'Yes'. [20]For no matter how many promises God has made, they are 'Yes' in Christ. And so through him the 'Amen' is spoken by us to the glory of God.

Continuing his defence, he turns now from his written to his spoken message (verses 18–19) which is, in summary, that *God is faithful* to his promises. Paul is affirming the same confidence in God as expressed by spokesmen from earlier generations, for example Balaam, who asked of God: 'Does he speak and then not act? Does he promise and not fulfil?'[6] Clearly Paul shared Balaam's belief in the faithfulness of God to his word. The numerous promises of God, given through the mouths of many prophets at different times and places,[7] all converge like so many lines at one point, the Son of God whom Paul and his companions now proclaim. There is no ambiguity, *Yes* and *No*, about the Son of God. It is as if God is saying 'Jesus Christ, my Son, is my "yes" to every promise I have ever made. He fulfils everything I have ever said.' From God's side, as well as from ours, everything is focused upon Christ and it is for this reason that the prepositions *in* and *through* are so important. Because God's promises come true *in* Christ, we say the *Amen* (Hebrew, 'it is true') *through* Christ *to the glory of God* (verse 20). Christ is the 'go-between'. God speaks to us *in* Christ and we, who have received the message, speak back to God *through* Christ. The apostle is teaching us that we may approach God by no other path and glorify him by no other means. Sin prevents us approaching God in our own right; but we may draw near *through* Christ.

Since Christ is the fulfilment (God's *Yes*) to all of God's numerous promises, it follows that the Old Testament, where the promises are made, really makes sense only when read with Christ in mind. Christ is the end to which the Old Testament is pointed, the goal toward which it moves.[8] To read the Old Testament without

[6] Nu. 23:19.   [7] *Cf.* Heb. 1:1–2.

[8] Rom. 10:4. For an excellent general discussion see G. Goldsworthy, *Gospel and Kingdom* (Paternoster, 1981).

reference to Christ is like reading a mystery novel with the final chapter torn out. All the clues are scattered throughout the story, but without the finale no-one could be sure of the explanation of the mystery or the identity of the one in whom all interest has been aroused. The gospel of the Son of God, as proclaimed by Paul, is the final chapter of God's story, which explains all, and without which everything which precedes remains enigmatic and 'up in the air'.

Paul shows us, in passing, what he thought of the old covenant. In defending his ministry against those who, having rejected the new covenant, sought to bring the Corinthians under the old, it would have been easy enough for Paul to over-react and reject it altogether. A little later he will say that the old is now fulfilled and outshone by the new covenant of Christ and the Spirit (3:7–11). Nevertheless the new covenant occurs only because of the promises made by God under the old covenant.[9] In our attitudes to the old covenant there are two extremes to avoid. On the one hand we may not treat the old as if the new covenant has not superseded it, as the newcomers were doing. On the other, we are not at liberty to dispense with it from our canon of Scripture as Marcion the Gnostic did a century later. What Paul teaches us is that the one God binds the new to the old covenant in one continuous self-disclosure which began in the book of Genesis and which reached its final and glorious revelation in the Son of God, Jesus Christ.

4. God is loyal to his people (1:21–22)

Now it is God who makes both us and you stand firm in Christ. He anointed us, [22]set his seal of ownership on us, and put his Spirit in our hearts as a deposit, guaranteeing what is to come.

Paul turns from the promises of God in the remote past to the present experience of the Corinthians. If God has proved faithful to his ancient promises he has also proved faithful in his present dealings with the Corinthians. Speaking to them as people who have heard and responded to the message of the Son of God, he assures them that God himself will keep them in their relationship with Christ. The word for *makes ... stand firm* was used in business law to signify a seller's guarantee to honour a contract. God is the guarantor of our life-long relationship with the Son of God. The present tense

[9] See further Rom. 1:2; 9:4; Lk. 24:44.

shows this to be no short-term guarantee but a permanent one.

What Paul looks forward to is the time when God will bring us into the physical presence of Jesus at the resurrection of all believers (4:14). The faithful God who is ensuring that we remain Christians until then gives us, in the meantime, the Holy Spirit who is described as a *seal* and a guarantee (verse 22).

The *seal* in antiquity was an impression made on wax by a special instrument (also called a seal) to indicate the ownership of a document. We continue to attach the company seal to important legal documents. The presence of the Holy Spirit within us is a seal of ownership. We should remember that we do not belong to ourselves but to God.[10] The 'guarantee' in Paul's day was a deposit or down-payment in pledge of payment in full. In modern Greek this word is also used of an engagement ring, which retains the idea of a guarantee or pledge of some greater thing which is yet to come. The greatest thing we look forward to is being gathered together with Christ at the resurrection (4:14), and to being transformed into the likeness of Christ in the meantime (3:18; 4:17).

How do we know we have the Holy Spirit dwelling *in our hearts*? In most (stable) families a child has the sense of belonging to his parents in their family. He not only bears their surname but also has an awareness that he is their child and they are his father and mother. Through the Holy Spirit God conveys to us the awareness that he is our Father and we are his children.[11] Only through the Holy Spirit do I have this filial awareness and confidence. Do I understand that God is my Father? If I do, then this is the evidence of the presence of the Holy Spirit within my life. The God who was faithful in keeping his promises made under the old covenant is also faithful and active in keeping me in relationship with Christ, and as a reassurance of his fidelity, he has given the Holy Spirit as a *seal* of ownership and guarantee of completed contract. The apostle will have much more to say about the Holy Spirit who is fundamental to the ministry and experience of the new covenant (3:3, 6, 17–18).

Paul does not explain where God's activity ends and ours begins. Elsewhere he teaches that while 'God works in' Christians, they must at the same time 'work out (their) salvation'.[12] This passage in 2 Corinthians, then, relieves us of no responsibilities. Rather, it sets before us the faithful activity of God in keeping us in our relationship with Christ. So far from allowing slackness, this is

---

[10] 1 Cor. 6:19–20.   [11] Rom. 8:14–16.   [12] Phil. 2:12–13.

intended to encourage a deepening relationship with Christ in the confidence that God is the source and the guarantee of that relationship.

We have now come almost to the end of Paul's first chapter of this letter. What he has written has been both autobiographical and theological. He has explained what has happened to him since he last saw them while also defending himself from criticism and misunderstanding. Yet he has also spoken about God in relationship to himself, and it is important to focus attention on this, since it might otherwise be misread. He does not write as an academic theologian but as a practical missionary and evangelist. He writes nothing about God which he has not experienced first hand in the realities of hardship and the crucible of suffering. Paul was afflicted; but God comforted him (verses 3–4). His life was, and continued to be, in danger; but God rescued him and would rescue him again, in answer to the prayers of the Corinthians (verses 9–11).

Now, in defending his own integrity, Paul has reminded the Corinthians that they are and will continue to be Christians because of the faithfulness of God. The God who made the promises has faithfully kept them in the coming of his Son, and it is this God who has 'commissioned' Paul and his companions to proclaim Jesus Christ the Son of God, in whom the Corinthians now believe. It is God who is keeping them in their relationship with Christ, though the Holy Spirit given as *seal* and guarantee.

The God who was faithful to his promise is also loyal to his people. Paul is a minister of this faithful God and of his new covenant. Let the Corinthians understand that, despite their criticisms of him, he too is faithful to them and loyal in his dealings with them.

While we should make every effort to keep to our arrangements and undertakings, occasions sometimes arise, as they had with Paul, where unforeseen circumstances make it difficult or impossible to do so. The harsh and critical attitudes of the Corinthians warn us how easy it is to react with only partial knowledge or with bitterness. Clearly our relationships to our friends, unlike those of the Corinthians, should be marked by sympathy, understanding, kindness and generosity.

1:23 – 2:13
3.   Why Paul changed his plans

During his recent emergency visit to Corinth Paul had told the Corinthians that he would pay them a return visit in the near future. Due to the force of circumstances, however, he had written them a letter – the so-called 'sorrowful' letter. He would now visit them at the end, not the beginning, of his itinerary. The change of plans certainly looked bad. Paul's reasons for delaying his return were, to put it briefly, to avoid further pain in his relationship with them.

1.   Reasons for not returning (1:23 – 2:2)

I call God as my witness that it was in order to spare you that I did not return to Corinth. ²⁴*Not that we lord it over your faith, but we work with you for your joy, because it is by faith you stand firm.* ^{2:1}*So I made up my mind that I would not make another painful visit to you.* ²*For if I grieve you, who is left to make me glad but you whom I have grieved?*

At some point back in Ephesus Paul *made up* his *mind* (verse 1) not to make another *painful visit* to Corinth. The verb he uses also means 'judged', implying careful consideration in arriving at this decision. He must have known that his failure to visit them would involve serious criticism of his character. Why, then, did he decide not to come?

It was, he writes, to *spare* them (verse 23) further grief (verse 2). Clearly the former visit had involved both Paul and the Corinthians in suffering (2:3), though what specifically had happened back in Corinth is not stated.

Our difficulty is that, while Paul and the Corinthians know what he is referring to, we today do not. The best we can do is to gather the bits and pieces of information in the letter and attempt to reconstruct the situation in Corinth.

It seems that the problem in Corinth had been caused by a particular man, as 2:5–9 suggests: 'if any*one* has caused grief, *he* has .... The punishment inflicted on *him* ... forgive and comfort *him* ...'. Paul speaks of 'the *one* who did the wrong' and 'the injured party' (7:12). Evidently a person in the Corinthian church had committed an act of aggression, immorality or injustice against another person.[1] Since Paul writes of a 'majority' who subsequently punished him (verse 6), we may suppose that a minority supported, and perhaps continued to support, the offender, possibly because he was an influential member of the Corinthian congregation.

Paul had undertaken his unscheduled visit to Corinth in an attempt to resolve the matter. It seems that while the majority agreed with Paul's views they were not prepared to take any action. This, apparently, was the context in which Paul inflicted 'pain' upon the Corinthians, though he does not say what he means. It may be significant that they also distressed him (2:3). Is he speaking of the pain involved in confronting the Corinthians with the need to take serious moral action which they were as yet unprepared to take and which has led to a sense of failure on their part and a sense of disappointment on his? It is difficult to be sure of the details but it seems clear that he is speaking about the pain of damaged relationships between himself and them.

Paul's method of dealing with this problem is interesting in establishing principles of pastoral relationships. Unlike the newcomers who 'enslave' them (11:20) Paul does not *lord it over* the Corinthians (verse 24). Jesus is their Lord; Paul is their servant (4:5), their 'co-worker' (1:24). Again, unlike the newcomers, he does not pretend to be self-sufficient (2:16; 3:4–6), but expresses his dependence upon them (verse 2). Although he is their apostle he also belongs to them (1:6).

On his return to Ephesus he came to realize that to revisit Corinth in the immediate future could only lead to more pain – both for them and for him. If the recent visit was unhelpful, would another one prove any different? Perhaps he is reflecting some of the insight of modern industrial relations procedures where, the negotiations having reached an impasse, it is better for the parties to separate for a cooling-off period to get things in perspective. The same principle

[1] For further discussion see comments on 7:5–16.

applies in strained marriage relationships where time for thinking rather than more talking is what is needed. Another visit, he now believed, could only make matters worse.

It is important to understand that he is doing much more than merely explaining and defending his actions. In expressing his dependence on them (verse 2) as one who *works with* them (verse 24), he is stating a fundamental principle of gospel relationships. He is not self-sufficient but dependent; and they are too. Moreover, he is open in disclosing his motives and reasons for not coming, which he says, have been worked out before God (1:23; *cf.* 1:12). If 'disguise' is the mark of his opponents, the false apostles (11:13), then openness is the mark of Paul, an openness which is made possible by the grace of God in forgiveness. If Paul is transparent, then, clearly, so too should the Corinthians be transparent. In embodying the gospel qualities of dependence and openness Paul shows himself to be the great Christian leader and teacher he was, continually modelling a godly lifestyle before the people.

2. The letter (2:3–4)

I wrote as I did so that when I came I should not be distressed by those who ought to make me rejoice. I had confidence in all of you, that you would all share my joy. ⁴For I wrote you out of great distress and anguish of heart and with many tears, not to grieve you but to let you know the depth of my love for you.

The letter to which he refers was written from Ephesus, but unfortunately it has not survived. It was delivered by Titus who brought their response to Paul in Macedonia. Paul will also refer to his letter in 7:8–13 where we will make further comments.

It should be noted that Paul wrote in the knowledge that the majority agreed with him (2:3), but were not prepared to take whatever action was necessary to deal with the wrongdoer. He did not write to achieve a fundamental change in their attitude to him or in their opinion of the matter in question. Confident of their loyalty he wrote in an attempt to secure a unified action towards the offender (7:12). Their lack of action against the wrongdoer was a barrier preventing the restoration of relationships between them and the apostle.

It was this restoration that Paul really sought. Their behaviour towards the offender was merely a means to that end (2:9; 7:12). What he wanted was that they *would all share* his *joy* (verse 3), which

45

could happen only when he and they shared the same moral perspectives in this matter. Paul's over-riding objective, therefore, was spiritual unity between them and him, a condition of which was a common mind towards the wrongdoer, expressed on their part by appropriate action.

Paul's lost letter was, apparently, deeply personal. The nature of the offence brought *great distress and anguish of heart* to him. He wrote *with many tears* to express *the depth of* his *love* for them and *not to grieve* them (verse 4). The writer was torn between his loving concern not to bring pain and his determination not to weaken godly standards for their congregational life.

Again, there is much to learn here about qualities of spiritual leadership which are so deeply needed at every level of church life. As we look at the whole passage (1:23 – 2:4) we see that Paul does not lord it over or dominate them; he works 'with' them (1:24). He loves them and tells them so (2:4b). Though they do not act in the way they should, he does not condemn them; he weeps with them (2:4a). He needs their ministry to him and tells them he needs it (2:2, 3a). He does not hold back from admonishing them (2:3). He is open about his motives and reasons, which he discloses to them (1:23). Our church life would be greatly enriched if, in our relationships with one another, Paul's principles of spiritual leadership were followed.

3. Forgive the man (2:5–11)

If anyone has caused grief, he has not so much grieved me as he has grieved all of you, to some extent — not to put it too severely. [6]*The punishment inflicted on him by the majority is sufficient for him.* [7]*Now instead, you ought to forgive and comfort him, so that he will not be overwhelmed by excessive sorrow.* [8]*I urge you, therefore, to reaffirm your love for him.* [9]*The reason I wrote you was to see if you would stand the test and be obedient in everything.* [10]*If you forgive anyone, I also forgive him. And what I have forgiven — if there was anything to forgive — I have forgiven in the sight of Christ for your sake,* [11]*in order that Satan might not outwit us. For we are not unaware of his schemes.*

This matter, whatever it was, had been the cause of spiritual suffering for the whole Corinthian congregation and doubtless also for Paul, deny it though he may (verse 5). And the cause of all this suffering has been just one man! What is the apostolic method of dealing with difficult customers or the openly immoral? So often the responsibility falls on the unfortunate pastor, so that it becomes a two-way power struggle between the offender and him. Here, however, the *majority* conveyed to the person what was probably the verdict of withdrawal from fellowship from him.[2] Paul calls it a *punishment* (verse 6). His policy has borne fruit; as a result of his letter the Corinthian church as a whole has dealt with the matter. The members have apparently come to realize that the offender has not only hurt Paul, he has hurt the whole church, such is its corporate nature (verse 5).[3] The 'sorrowful' letter has achieved what the 'painful' visit failed to achieved – a clear-cut unified response among the Corinthians (7:11).

The corporate nature of Christianity comes out clearly in the passage. Paul's words are addressed not only to individuals, but also to the church whose members minister to one another by their gifts.[4] Lively and open relationships provide the best context for the word of God to work out its purposes among us. This is why the local congregation is so highly regarded and referred to as 'the church of God' (1:1).

Therefore he exhorts them to restore the now-penitent man. They are to *forgive and comfort him* (verse 7) and express their *love for him* (verse 8). Further, they are able to reassure him that Paul also forgives him, which he is able to do, despite his deep feelings *in the sight of Christ* (verse 10). This unusual expression may mean the ability to forgive someone only through one's relationship with Christ. Now that the matter has been resolved it is important that the man should be restored in his relationships with them. Paul's forgiveness of the man was, he states, *for* their *sake* (verse 10) that is, *in order that Satan might not outwit us* (verse 11). Satan, who is ever ready to destroy churches, will, in the absence of love and forgiveness, quickly bring bitterness and division. Now that the man has turned from his evil ways it is important that he, and the group who support him, be reconciled through forgiveness with the main body of the congregation.

4. Paul in Troas (2:12–13)

Now when I went to Troas to preach the gospel of Christ and found that the Lord had opened a door for me, [13]I still had no peace of mind, because I did not find my brother Titus there. So I said goodbye to them and went on to Macedonia.

---

[2] 1 Cor. 5:11.   [3] See 1 Cor. 12:26.   [4] 1 Cor. 12:7–11.

a. The rendezvous: Troas

Paul arranged to meet Titus in Troas to hear how the Corinthians had responded to his letter. Since he speaks of coming to Troas *to preach the gospel of Christ* (verse 12), it may be that he had been planning for some time to come there for that purpose. His forced withdrawal from Ephesus had provided him with the opportunity to do so. Troas, then, would be the place to which Titus was to bring the Corinthians' reply to Paul. (The arrangement appears to have been that if Titus had not come before winter closed the seas to shipping they would meet in Macedonia.)

Troas, although scarcely mentioned by surviving documents of the ancient world, appears in the New Testament as a transit city for travel between northern Greece and Asia Minor, as recent scholarship has shown.[5] Paul's earlier visit to Troas had .been remarkable for two reasons. According to Acts it was at Troas that Luke joined Paul's company for the first time, as may be noticed in the change of pronouns from 'they' to 'we'.[6] It was also at Troas that the 'Macedonian man' appeared to Paul in a vision bidding him to 'Come over ... and help us.'[7] From Troas, then, Paul and his companions departed to Macedonia, and from there to Achaia, and its capital, Corinth. When Paul writes of saying *goodbye to them* (verse 13), it is clear that there were at least some Christians in Troas.

b. An open door and a restless spirit

The 'opened door' happily matched his intention in coming to Troas which was (literally) 'for *the gospel of Christ*' (verse 12). God opened the door of opportunity at Troas. Other references also speak of God opening doors for Christian ministry.[8]

Paul, however, was so preoccupied with the Corinthians and their likely attitudes to the letter that he *had no peace of mind* (literally 'spirit', verse 13). Although the reason he gives for this restlessness is that he *did not find* his *brother Titus there*, he means us to understand that concern for the Corinthians was the chief source of his anxiety. This is another example of Paul laying bare his inner emotional life to the Corinthians (*cf.* 1:8; 2:4). It is possible that Paul makes these disclosures deliberately so that the readers will

[5] Acts 16:8, 11; 20:5–6; 2 Tim. 4:13. C. J. Hemer, 'Alexandrian Troas', *Tyndale Bulletin* 26 (1975), pp. 79–112.
[6] Acts 16:11.   [7] Acts 16:8–9.   [8] Acts 14:27; Col. 4:3.

understand the reality of his weakness, as opposed to the dazzling image of powerful self-sufficiency projected by his opponents. He wants people to relate to him as he is (12:6b), and to understand that if he prevails it is not in his own power, but God's (4:7; 12:9–10). This has something to say to the minister or church leader who is tempted to engage in image-making as practised by media-conscious advertisers and politicians. For Paul, integrity (4:2) and reality, even reality about weakness, were fundamental to the gospel.

His zeal for the gospel brought him to Troas, but his passionate concern for the Corinthians kept him from staying there, despite the opportunities for preaching the gospel which now existed. Significantly, Paul revisited Troas a year later when finally withdrawing from the region. On that occasion he remained for seven days.[9] Perhaps God kept the door open?

c. My brother Titus

While Paul regarded all believers as 'brothers', some enjoyed a special relationship with him. Epaphras, for example, who evangelized the Colossians, is spoken of as 'our dear fellow-servant'.[10] Titus, in all probability converted through Paul, enjoyed a close relationship with the apostle. He will refer to him as 'my partner and fellow worker' in his labours among the Corinthians (8:23). God had given Titus, like Paul, a deep and affectionate concern for the Corinthians (8:16; 7:15).

In this letter Paul reveals how dejected he had been – in Ephesus (1:8), in Troas (2:13) and in Macedonia (7:5). When God restored Paul it was by means of the arrival of his good friend Titus and through his encouragement. If we would be used by God to 'comfort the downcast' (7:6), it will be important to give ourselves in loyal and encouraging friendship to others. Loyal Christian friends are treasure beyond price; Titus is an admirable model.

Paul's pastoral strategy is illuminating. As well as his public ministry to congregations, it is evident that he devoted special attention to key individuals such as Titus, Archippus, Timothy and Luke.[12] By a sustained one-to-one fellowship Paul was able to multiply his ministry through these able fellow workers. Modern

---

[9] Acts 20:6.   [10] Col. 1:7.   [11] Tit. 1:4.
[12] See E. E. Ellis, 'Paul and his Co-workers', *NTS* 17 (1971), pp. 437–452.

pastors can readily adapt this principle by setting aside a few hours a week for concentrated ministry to key or needy individuals.

What happened next? On arriving in Macedonia, did he find Titus? How had the Corinthians responded to the letter? Having aroused our interest, Paul, for reasons that are unclear, leaves us in suspense. Rather, he will engage in a long digression about the apostolic ministry of the new covenant. Not until 7:5 will he resume his narrative and say what happened when he came to Macedonia.

II The ministry of the new covenant (2:14 – 7:4)

2:14 – 3:6
4. Opposition in Corinth

Paul now introduces the shadowy figures of his newly arrived opponents, whom he refers to as *many* (2:17) and as *some* who *need letters of recommendation* (3:1). At no time in the letter does he address them directly. It appears from what he writes that they have made many criticisms about Paul to the Corinthians. He is, they complain, an incompetent person, always running away from his problems and showing no sign of possessing the power of God. Furthermore, he has no-one but himself to commend his ministry; he is merely self-commended. They, by comparison, are self-sufficient, possessed of the power of God and commended by letter for their ministry. In the passage that follows Paul makes his reply to these criticisms.

1. Paul and the peddlers (2:14–17)

But thanks be to God, who always leads us in triumphal procession in Christ and through us spreads everywhere the fragrance of the knowledge of him. [15] *For we are to God the aroma of Christ among those who are being saved and those who are perishing.* [16] *To the one we are the smell of death; to the other, the fragrance of life. And who is equal to such a task?* [17] *Unlike so many, we do not peddle the word of God for profit. On the contrary, in Christ we speak before God with sincerity, like men sent from God.*

a. Triumphalism

The word *triumphal* is critical in this section. It may be that the new teachers in Corinth presented themselves as sweeping all before them as they triumphantly captured the Gentile churches for Moses

51

and the old covenant (*cf.* 10:13–15). To them, Paul with his recent reversals in Corinth and Ephesus and with his message of a crucified Messiah, was a sorry, defeated figure, the embodiment of weakness compared with their self-sufficient power.

The first part of the 'long digression' (2:14 – 3:6) is particularly important. Paul tells the Corinthians, in vivid language, how he sees his ministry in terms of its inner reality. Let the Corinthians and the newcomers understand that so far from abject defeat God was actually leading him in a victory procession – and this regardless of rejection in Corinth, expulsion from Ephesus, turmoil in Troas and anxiety in Macedonia. Even in what appeared to be reversal and difficulty he was being *led* by *God*, a matter for which he gives *thanks* (verse 14).[1]

The general picture in verse 14a is of a Roman victory procession, though Paul's specific point is somewhat uncertain, as witnessed by the variety of suggestions as to the precise meaning.[2] Military leaders were granted a public victory procession (*triumphas*) through Rome only after winning major battles. The most spectacular procession of the first century was the celebration of the conquest of the Jews when, in AD 71, the Emperor Vespasian and his son Titus rode in chariots through the streets of Rome behind their pathetic prisoners of war. Josephus, the Jewish historian, records this at length,[3] and it also depicted on the Titus Arch in Rome, where it may still be seen. It is not clear whether Paul sees himself as the conquering general or as his captive. A case can be made for both, though the apostle as a captive slave seems more likely. Whatever he meant, we can be sure that, despite the appearance of weakness, it was God who *always* and *everywhere* led Paul in triumphal procession (verse 14).

This was not, however, the triumphalism of Paul's opponents, who declared themselves superior to Paul in missionary success as well as in ecstatic experience. Success and strength were the marks as well as the objectives of their ministry and significant numbers of the Corinthians came under their influence.

Christian triumphalism, although a contradication in terms, has had its appeal in many subsequent generations. The Emperor

---

[1] See also 1:11; 4:15; 8:16; 9:15 for other references to thanksgiving, a profoundly important practice for Paul.

[2] *E.g.* P. Marshall, 'A Metaphor of Social Shame', *Nov. Test.* 15/4 (1983), pp. 302-317, by an interesting parallel in Seneca, suggests that the imagery denotes social shame.

[3] *Jewish War* vii, 132–157.

Constantine believed that he won his greatest battle through the first two Greek letters of Christ's name which were inscribed, cross-like, on the shields of his soldiers. Many subsequent Christian leaders have sought victory in battle in and for the name of Christ. In the Middle Ages it was believed that God was glorified through soaring cathedrals and spectacular church ceremony. Closer to our own times there have been some expressions of missionary work in under-developed countries which appear to have been as much inspired by a spirit of colonial expansion and cultural superiority as by obedience to the Great Commission of Christ. In our own century, triumphalist language has been used of some church-growth movements and the development of the so-called 'great churches'.

For his part, Paul consistently applies anti-triumphalist language to his ministry throughout this letter. He is the Corinthians' servant, a dying man, 'weak' and a fool.[4] The newcomers' ministry, like their Christ, was characterized by a this-worldly triumphalism. His ministry, like his Christ, was characterized by crucifixion. This has serious implications for the way Christians think and speak about their faith.

'Triumphalism' in all its forms is excluded by the studied remarks of the apostle Paul within this letter. What is important to God is not 'bigness' – of church buildings, or of the numbers who gather there – but faithful and sacrificial service, based on the example of Christ himself.

b. Fragrance

The burning of incense along the victory route was part of the ceremonial of the Roman triumph. The sense of smell, as well as of sight and hearing, was involved in the splendour of the occasion. As Paul was led by God, so too (to continue the imagery of the victory procession), Paul *spreads everywhere* a *fragrance* (verse 14). Although he rejects triumphalism, his ministry is not without effect. If incense impinges on the senses, even though invisible, so too Paul's ministry makes its presence felt.

If a fragrance is smelt, so a person is known. What God does through Paul and his companions is to *spread ... the knowledge* of God *everywhere* (verse 14). The *'knowledge of God'* in biblical thought is not

[4] 2 Cor. 4:5, 11; 11:29; 12:11.

53

nearly so abstract or intellectual as it sounds. For instance, when we read that 'Adam *knew* Eve his wife' (Gn. 4:1, AV, RSV) something as physical as sexual intercourse is in mind. If 'knowing' one's wife is a real experience, so too 'knowing' God is a real though different inter-personal experience. What God was doing through Paul was establishing relationships between himself and people. Paul's evangelism, therefore, although non-triumphalist, was nevertheless effective and noticeable. Later, he will remind them that 'the weapons we fight with ... have divine power' (10:4–5).

c. Life and death

Paul pursues the imagery of fragrance, though he changes it from the incense of the Roman triumph to the *aroma* associated with the burnt offerings of the book of Leviticus.[5] Although an aroma of sacrifice is unseen, its presence is unmistakable in the nostrils of the worshipper. The point of the metaphor is that, although the *word of God* (verse 17) is also invisible, there is no doubting its effects. It divides its hearers into two groups; *those who are being saved* and *those who are perishing* (verse 15). For those who receive the *word of God* the message is *the fragrance of life*, but for those who reject it there is *the smell of death*.

To some, the gospel is just a message about a defeated, dead man which they reject in the same way a person would recoil from the odour of a decomposing corpse. These people are *perishing*, as dead in principle as they perceive Christ to be. To others, however, the message is about the risen Christ which they receive in the way a person welcomes the fragrance of a beautiful perfume. These people are being saved; they are as alive in principle as they perceive Christ to be. Although, being sinners, they are on their way to death, because of the presence of the Holy Spirit within their lives they look forward to life beyond death.[6]

It is no surprise, therefore, that Paul could have felt embarrassed by a message which proved to be so divisive. Those who recoiled from the Christ of whom Paul spoke doubtless also recoiled from the speaker. It is for this reason Paul refers in this letter to 'troubles ... beatings, imprisonments' and to experiencing 'dishonour' and 'bad report' and to being 'regarded as imposters' (6:4, 8). While we do

[5] *E.g.* Lv. 2:12.
[6] *Cf.* Rom. 8:10–11.

not seek rejection or unpopularity, it may be our lot to suffer these things as a result of faithful ministry of the gospel.

How did Paul feel when his hearers did not receive the word of God? It is apparent that he made strong efforts to persuade people to respond positively to his message.[7] He was convinced it was God who appealed to people to 'be reconciled to God' (5:20). John Calvin wrestled with the problem of rejection of the message when he commented on our passage: 'The gospel is preached unto salvation, for that is its real purpose ... The proper function of the gospel is always to be distinguished from its accidental function which must always be imputed to the depravity of men by which life is turned into death.'

Jesus wept over Jerusalem even though its people would demand his death.[8] Paul experienced 'great sorrow and unceasing anguish' towards his fellow Jews even though they had caused him such heartache and suffering.[9] Do we weep like Jesus or, like Paul, feel deep anguish about the indifference of our fellow countrymen towards Christ?

d. The message and the man

Paul was keenly aware of the close relationship between the message and the messenger who brought it. On the one hand he states that *we speak ... like men sent from God* (verse 17), and on the other he writes that *we are to God the aroma of Christ* (verse 15). It is *through us*, he says, that God *spreads ... the fragrance of the knowledge of* God (verse 14). The sacrificial lifestyle of the messenger is an extension of the ministry and death of Jesus himself. It is not too much to say that the message about Christ is encountered and received (or rejected) in the person of the messenger. The message incarnated in the messenger is a fragrance of life to those who obey it, but to others it has the odour of death. Barrett comments that 'the apostles are the smoke that arises from the sacrifice of Christ to God'.

The notion that others reach their decisions about Christ, for salvation or destruction, on account of those in whom the message is embodied is so onerous that Paul exclaims: *Who is equal to such a task?* (verse 16). Later he will reply to his question with the affirmation, 'our competence comes from God' (3:5).

Governments take great care in the appointment of their ambas-

[7] 2 Cor. 5:11; *cf.* Acts 17:2–4.   [8] Lk. 19:41.   [9] Rom. 9:2.

sadors for the good reason that nations are judged by those who represent them. It is both a privilege and a responsibility to act on behalf of one's country. But, as Paul knew well, it is far more serious to represent the Lord.

The twentieth century has witnessed a communications revolution which has made the world a 'global village'. Missionary and evangelistic agencies exploit modern technology in, for example, gospel recordings, radio and television ministries, audio-visuals, cassettes and video recorders. While there are clear benefits, there is also the danger that our ministries become impersonal, using 'things' and treating people like 'things'. By using the technology, is it possible that we Christians become just another depersonalizing and alienating force within the community? Moreover, do we not sometimes find the commitment of ourselves as persons to other persons too high a price to pay? It seems easier to deliver a hundred church leaflets to letterboxes than to get to know just one person. When we depersonalize the gospel we rob it of its intrinsically human character. How important, therefore, to keep the balance between *speaking* the word of God and *being* the aroma of Christ.

e. The 'many'

Paul now mentions for the first time his opponents, who will reappear throughout the letter.[10] His lack of reference to them in those sections which refer to the 'painful' visit and the 'sorrowful' letter[11] suggests they had not yet arrived in Corinth at the time of Paul's 'painful' visit. They appear to have arrived since then, so Paul would have known them only through the report of Titus.

Paul now places the ministries of these newcomers side by side with his own. They – *many*, implying a group – both adulterate and profit from the *word of God* (verse 17). The verb used of these 'peddlers' was used of wine hawkers who watered down the pure vintage to make fraudulent profits. The implication is that these persons were receiving (excessive?) payment from the Corinthians in return for a diluted, weakened message.

The *word of God* refers to the spoken word of the Christian gospel, as declared by the apostles.[12] Although Paul exercised some freedom to emphasize this point or that, depending on the understanding of

[10] 2 Cor. 3:1; 4:2; 5:12; chs. 10 – 13 *passim*.   [11] 2 Cor. 1:23 – 2:11; 7:5–16.
[12] *Cf.* 1 Thes. 2:13.

his audience, there was nevertheless a definable content to the message.[13] While significant differences of opinion existed between Peter, Paul and James,[14] when it came to the gospel message that 'Christ died for our sins' and 'was raised on the third day', Paul emphasizes their fundamental agreement by stating, 'this is what we preach, and this is what you believed'.[15] It was from the 'word of God', whose content was defined by the apostles, that these peddlers were departing. Later he will complain that they proclaim another Jesus and a different gospel (11:4). Since the 'word of God', which they are altering, has a definite content, Paul's complaint about the newcomers is neither petty nor personal, but objective.

If objectively he points to deficiencies in their message, subjectively Paul makes much of his own integrity. In what follows (chapters 3 – 6), he will explain and expand upon the 'word of God' as it applies to the Corinthians. At this point he is at pains to establish that he speaks *with sincerity, like men sent from God* and *before God* (verse 17). In response to the new ministers who focus attention on such visible things as letters of recommendation, ecstatic utterance, visions and miracles, Paul invites the Corinthians to examine his integrity and sincerity.

The comparison throughout the letter of his inner and their outer qualities is well summarized by the contrast he makes between 'what is seen' (literally someone's 'face') and 'the heart' (5:12). If the newcomers seek to authenticate their ministry by the appearance of things, by 'face', Paul is defending himself in respect of his 'heart'. In speaking *with sincerity* (literally, 'tested by the sun') he wants the Corinthians to know that he, for his part, was not exercising his ministry for financial or any other kind of gain. Moreover, unlike the newcomers whose authorization is no higher than those whose commendatory letters they bear, Paul's ministry originated with God, a reference to the Damascus Road event when he was commissioned to go to the Gentiles with the message centred *in Christ*.

Paul knew, as well as they, that his claims to *sincerity* and to being *sent from God* were easily discounted as just his opinions. His defence is that he speaks *before God*, in the presence of God. He wants the Corinthians to know that he lived every day as if it was the day of judgment, hence his references to 'before God' and 'in the sight of

---

[13] Compare Acts 13:16–41 (to Jews) with 17:22–31 (to Gentiles).
[14] Gal. 1:6–9.   [15] 1 Cor. 15:3–4, 11.

God' used elsewhere in the letter.[16] All that he says, does and above all, thinks is 'plain to God'.[17]

Not that Paul's invisible fellowship with God lacks visible evidence. The reality of his apostolic call and of his inner relationship with God may be discerned in the effects of his ministry. God *spreads*, or more literally 'manifests', ... *the knowledge of* God through Paul (verse 14). The Corinthian Christians themselves *show*, or again more literally 'manifest', that they are 'a letter from Christ' to be known and read by their fellow Corinthians (3:2–3). Although he emphasizes his inner or 'heart' relationship with God, they may, nevertheless, be 'proud' that he is actively 'persuading' people to become Christians (5:11; *cf.* 1:14). In the words of Jesus, the genuineness of Paul's ministry may be recognized by his 'fruit'.[18]

Although Paul's commission by God was unique, and the dispute between the newcomers and himself an unrepeatable fact of history, there is an ongoing application from these verses. It is that those who engage in ministry must speak only the 'word of God' and they must do so 'before God'. The newcomers' style of ministry warns us of the ever-present temptation for ministers to project and to commend themselves on the basis of 'image', or what Paul calls 'face'. While the minister needs gifts appropriate to his calling, let him come not in the strength of those gifts but in the power of the word of God.

2. Their letters (3:1)

Are we beginning to commend ourselves again? Or do we need, like some people, letters of recommendation to you or from you?

Paul's difficulty was that he lacked external accreditation. He was not one of the original disciples of Jesus. The Corinthians had only Paul's word that he was in good standing with the leaders of the Jerusalem church.[19] His only course was to reiterate that the risen Lord had called him to be an apostle and to point to his sacrificial lifestyle as legitimizing that call. Yet this easily made it appear that he was 'commending himself'.[20] His dilemma was that he must

[16] 2 Cor. 4:2; *cf.* 5:11–12; 12:19.
[17] 2 Cor. 5:11; *cf.* 1:12, 14, 23. [18] Mt. 7:20.
[19] Gal. 2:9.
[20] Here, as usual, it is the plural 'we' by which he includes his co-workers.

either say nothing in his defence and allow the work in Corinth to be destroyed by default, or run the risk of the accusation that he was blowing his own trumpet. According to Goudge, 'Self-defence is almost impossible without self-commendation. St. Paul's opponents made the former necessary, and then blamed him for the latter.'

Although he does not answer his own question directly, the implications is that he was not, in fact, commending himself. If he will commend himself it is to their 'consciences' and then 'in the sight of God' (4:2). He knew that it is the Lord who commends a person, not the person himself (10:18), and that the commendation is directed towards the consciences of others. Although he does not commend himself, he feels deeply that the Corinthians should have commended him (12:11), since he was in no way inferior to his opponents, not even in their much vaunted field of 'signs, wonders and miracles' (12:12). Nevertheless he does remind them of the facts. It is through him that God manifests the fragrance of the knowledge of God, and it is by his ministry that the Christians in Corinth manifest that they are a letter from Christ to the watching world.

Paul's opponents based their claims on *letters of recommendation* (verse 1). At that time such letters were common, and Paul himself used letters to introduce people to new congregations.[21] So who wrote these letters commending the newcomers to the Corinthians? This is one of the major unanswered questions of the New Testament. Since they were 'Hebrews' (11:22), it is likely that the commendation came from a Jewish quarter. It has been suggested that the letters came from James, the leader of the Jerusalem church.[22]

Against this suggestion it is noted that Paul does not say that the letters came from James, which presumably he would have done. Moreover, it is unlikely that Paul would have persevered with the famine relief collection and taken it to Jerusalem,[23] had these persons, who were bent on destroying Paul's ministry in Corinth, in fact been sent by James. Again, if James had been the source of the commendation, why would these persons also need letters *from* the Corinthians (verse 1)? The great name of the Lord's brother would surely have been sufficient. The most likely suggestion is that the signatories were extreme Judaistic Christians in Jerusalem whose

---

[21] Rom. 16:1; 2 Cor. 8:22; Col. 4:7–8.
[22] *Cf.* Gal. 2:12.   [23] Acts 21:17; 24:17.

emissaries, probably without James's support,[24] had embarked on a misguided programme of capturing Paul's churches for their own brand of Jewish Christianity. The fact that these newcomers also seek letters *from* the Corinthians indicates that they intended to use Corinth as a springboard to other Pauline churches (10:13–16). When he writes later that 'they measure themselves by themselves and compare themselves with themselves' (10:12), he may mean that the senders and their messengers belong to the same group and that there is no higher commending authority in whose name they may come.

Whoever the letters are from, Paul says he does not need them,[25] as he now proceeds to explain.

3. Paul's letter (3:2)

You yourselves are our letter, written on our hearts, known and read by everybody.

Imagine the reactions when the Corinthian church assembled for the reading of Paul's most recent letter. The newcomers have letters of recommendation; Paul says he had no need of them. What, then, will he say? To what will he point to justify his ministry? As the reader read Paul's next words aloud, the Corinthian assembly must have been somewhat shaken to hear him say, *You yourselves are our letter* (verse 2). He will not point to a great person or persons whom he represents or in whose name he comes. Rather, he will stake his claim to legitimate ministry on the existence of the Corinthian church.

Prior to Paul's coming, there was no Christian community in Corinth. Through his labours there was now a congregation in that large and prosperous city, some of whose members had been criminals and immoral people.[26] In the first letter (9:1–2) he referred to the Corinthian church as 'the result of my work in the Lord' and 'the seal of my apostleship'. If the Corinthians need evidence that Paul was a true apostle let them look at themselves: *You yourselves are our letter* (verse 2).

According to Adolph Deissmann, correspondence in those times was classifiable as either private (a 'letter') or public (an 'epistle').[27]

---

[24] See Acts 15:24.

[25] The form of verse 1b in Greek is that of a rhetorical question expecting the answer 'No'.

[26] 1 Cor. 6:9–11.

[27] *Light from the Ancient East* (Hodder and Stoughton, 1909), pp. 224–246. For critical discussion of Deissmann see R. N. Longenecker, 'The Forms, Function and Authority of the

Although Deissmann took the opposite view, what Paul wrote to the churches were 'epistles', deliberately composed for reading in public. As his letter to Colosse was also to be read in Laodicea, so too the (lost) letter to Laodicea was to be read in Colosse.[28] John's seven letters to the churches in Asia Minor were to be incorporated in a book which was to be sent to and read in the seven churches.[29] The 'letter' written in the lives of the Corinthians was, like the letter written to them, a public document, an 'epistle', able to be *known and read by everybody* (verse 2).

The 'letter' which the world at large reads, Paul also reads, but inwardly, since it is *written on our*[30] *hearts*. When he brought the Christian message to Corinth he came to know many of the people in a personal way. He regarded himself as their father; he had them in his heart (6:11–13). The reformed fornicators, homosexuals, thieves and drunkards of whom he spoke[31] were real persons with names and faces. If he taught in public he also spoke to such people in private.[32] It is unlikely that the new lifestyle of the Corinthians was accomplished easily, smoothly or without disappointment. The letter of the Corinthian Christians was read by all, but it was also *written on* Paul's *heart*, the Greek perfect tense indicating that they were permanently engraved there.

The test of true ministry to which Paul had submitted himself is one which other ministers can apply to themselves. It is one thing to possess the appropriate ordination documents or the framed university degree proudly displayed; but are there 'living' letters? The confirmation of one's ministry lies in the effects of that ministry in human lives. This will depend upon having ministered a pure, undiluted gospel and also upon having taken people into our hearts. To do the former alone could mean inflexibility, while to do the latter alone could mean sentimentality. The proper balance lies in faithfulness to the gospel and pastoral love of the people.

4. Christ's letter (3:3)

You show that you are a letter from Christ, the result of our ministry, written not with ink but with the Spirit of the living God, not on tablets of stone but on tablets of human hearts.

New Testament Letters', in *Scripture and Truth*, ed. D. Carson and J. Woodbridge (IVP, 1983), pp.101–114.   [28] Col. 4:16.   [29] Rev. 1:11; 22:18.
[30] The reading 'our' (NIV) as opposed to 'your' (RSV) has better manuscript support.
[31] 1 Cor. 6:11.   [32] *Cf.* Acts 20:20.

What value had the newcomers' letters of recommendation in establishing their credentials as true ministers of God? At best the letters came with the authority of church leaders elsewhere; at worst they carried the names of persons from their own faction, making the newcomers their own sources of commendation.

Paul had a letter of recommendation – the Christian Corinthians. But whose name began this letter? To which higher authority does Paul appeal for recommendation? *You*, he informs them, *are a letter from Christ*. Christ, the author and source of the new lifestyle of the Corinthians, authenticates and legitimizes Paul's ministry. The letter from Christ was *the result of* Paul's *ministry*. Because the conversion of the Corinthians had its source and origin in Christ it was evident that Paul was his 'minister'.

So Paul does have tangible attestation for his ministry. What better proof could be produced than people whose lives are so radically changed? What, by comparison, is a mere letter *written with ink* on a piece of paper? 'Paul's credentials', comments C. F. D. Moule, 'are not on paper but in persons.'[33]

Nevertheless, what is now 'manifest' (verse 3, RV) for all to read was first written in their *hearts* with the *Spirit of the living God*. The new lifestyle which was so visible and striking was the outworking of something which began within the inner recesses of their hearts, through the power of the Spirit of God. True Christianity is not a veneer of morality glued on to the exterior of our lives, but a profound change of heart, mind and will which is then expressed in outward behaviour. The word of God changes individuals, in the context of Christian fellowship, from the inside out.

The ministry of the newcomers, supported as it is by ink on paper, really belongs to the now superseded covenant of Moses which was written on *tablets of stone* (verse 3). In contrast to the power of the *living God*, that ministry is now a dead letter, utterly incapable of transforming people. Moses' epoch is now passed; it is gone for ever, overtaken by the new age of Christ and the Spirit. The new missionaries hopelessly attempt to turn the clock back. But it is too late. The new covenant of Christ, in which Paul is a minister, imparts the Spirit to the inner recesses of the heart and brings a new creation.

Paul's words encourage pastors to persevere at, and give priority

[33] '2 Cor. 3:18b', in *Neues Testament und Geschichte*, ed. H. Baltensweiler and B. Reicke (Tübingen, 1972), p. 232.

to, the word of God. They should not deprive themselves of the reassurance which comes from seeing the effects of faithful ministry. Organizational and adminstrative matters have their place, but they are peripheral and not at the centre of that ministry by which Christ changes lives from the inside out. It is also helpful for a congregation to have a clear understanding of the nature of ministry and to encourage their minister to follow biblical priorities for his pastoral work.

5. Confidence and competence (3:4–5)

Such confidence as this is ours through Christ before God. Not that we are competent to claim anything for ourselves, but our competence comes from God.

The challenge from Corinth had apparently forced Paul to engage in some soul-searching. Was it after all just his opinion against that of the newcomers? What right had he to claim to be a minister of the long-awaited new covenant? Was he perhaps too confident in his theological judgment? Did his achievements merely flow from his own innate zeal and ability? Yet he cannot deny what had happened to these people. He has *confidence* that these things have actually taken place, although it has nothing to do with his own personal *competence* (verse 4). He has not measured himself against his opponents and declared himself to be superior. His *confidence*, significantly, is directed towards *God* (verse 4). Paul, it seems, has laid himself and all he has done before God and he has been able, in his conscience, to declare his ministry to belong to the new covenant, to be true and acceptable to God. He makes it clear, however, that he does not minister before God or draw near to God in his own right or in his own name. It is only *through Christ* that he has this confidence before God.

The three occurences of *competence* or *competent* (verses 5–6) refer back to his question: 'Who is equal to such a task? (2:16). It appears that here too he is engaging in debate with his opponents. Their claim, apparently, was to powerful self-sufficiency. They regarded Paul as weak and lacking the resources of a true minister. In agreeing with them Paul indicates that what he is engaged in is not his own project but God's. Yet, by his words, though a mere man, Paul 'saves' or 'destroys' others. Through his ministry the Spirit of God fundamentally changes other human lives. Can anyone have the power, the resources or the *competence*, to do these things? The answer must be no; only God himself can be the source of such things. Of and from himself he has no *competence*, no 'sufficiency' (RV; RSV). His competence, like his commission, is *from God*.

The ministry of Paul and all who have subsequently become ministers of the new covenant is not offered for the approval of man but for the endorsement of God. It was *before God* that Paul had his *confidence*. Nor does the strength which all ministers of the word of God need come from within themselves. Ministers of the gospel will say with Paul, *our competence comes from God*.

6. The new covenant (3:6)

He has made us competent as ministers of a new covenant – not of the letter but of the Spirit; for the letter kills, but the Spirit gives life.

a. The new covenant: the Spirit

There are two features of Paul's response to the new ministers in Corinth – subjective and objective. It is important that they are reminded of his personal character, that he is a person of integrity, called by God and made *competent* by God for the ministry of the word of God. The confirmation of his apostleship, however, lies not in himself, his powers or resources, but in the effects of his ministry in people, effects which have their origin in Christ (see verse 3).

Objectively, Paul states that his opponents are altering the fundamentals of the faith; they are adulterating the word of God. He now turns and explains that word more fully, as it applies to the Corinthians in their present situation. Above all it is vital that they understand that the promises of the old covenant are fulfilled by Christ (1:20) and the coming of the Spirit.

Within a few verses he mentions two prominent Old Testament promises which have been realized within the experience of the Corinthians. His references in verse 3 to the Spirit, tablets of stone and human hearts call to mind Ezekiel's words: 'I will remove from you your heart of stone and give you a heart of flesh. And I will put my Spirit in you.'[34] Then, in verse 6, he refers to *a new covenant*, which Jeremiah prophesied: '"The time is coming," declares the Lord, "when I will make a new covenant ... It will not be like the

[34] Ezk. 36:26–27.

covenant I made with their forefathers.'"[35] From his vantage point Paul sees both promises focused on Christ and the Spirit of God. He combines the prophecies of Ezekiel and Jeremiah into one statement and refers to *a new covenant ... of the Spirit*.

Paul's remarkable claim is that God has made him 'competent' to be a *minister* of the *new covenant*, a claim which is open to investigation and verification. There is no doubt that such promises were made. The question is: Were these Corinthian experiences of Christ and the Spirit identifiable with the ancient promises? Therefore we ask: Had these people experienced the forgiveness of sins as promised by Jeremiah? Was the law of God now written within their hearts as Jeremiah and Ezekiel said it would be? The answer to these questions is in the affirmative. Such is the transformation of their lives that Paul is able to refer to them as 'a new creation' (5:17), a people in whose hearts the light of God has shone (4:6). Let the Corinthians understand that the long-awaited new covenant has come and that, through the ministry of Paul, they have entered it.

b. The old covenant: death

He contrasts this new covenant with the old covenant, a covenant *of the letter*, which, he says, *kills*. He does not say that the law kills. (The word 'law', in fact, does not appear within 2 Corinthians.) Elsewhere he wrote that 'the law is holy, and the commandment is holy, righteous and good'.[36] Moreover, Jeremiah prophesied that in the new covenant the law will be written upon the hearts of the people. The new covenant, therefore, does not abolish the law; it establishes it in the only place it will be effective – in the heart. Under the old covenant the people did not have the spiritual resources to keep the law, or any provision for forgiveness when they broke it. The law became a finger of accusation pointed against them. Until the law had been internalized through the Spirit it remained the 'letter', an instrument which 'kills'.

These Hebrew newcomers, apparently, sought to impose the old covenant upon these Gentile Corinthian Christians. While they proclaimed Jesus and the Spirit, it was another Jesus and a different spirit (11:4), though what exactly they did teach, Paul does not say. What is clear is that, in seeking to impose the old covenant upon the

[35] Je. 31:31ff. [36] Rom. 7:12; *cf.* 3:21.

65

Corinthians, they did not accept the radical nature, the newness, of the new covenant, or the power of the Spirit of God. Paul, however, recognized that what they advocated would mean a retreat from life back into death, as he proceeds to explain.

c. The covenant is with a people

It is important for us to understand that the covenant God makes is not so much with individuals in a private religious sense, as with a people. If the 'long digression' begins with a reference to a 'new covenant' (3:6) it concludes with God's appeal to 'my *people*' (6:16). Through the ministry of the word of God these Corinthians have become members of a new covenant of God's people. Moreover, Paul does not speak of *the* new covenant as if quite different from the old. It is *a* new covenant, that is, a new phase of the one great covenant of God with his people which is the subject of the Bible's story. Thus the Corinthian Christians, who were mostly Gentiles, were to regard the ancient Hebrews as their forefathers,[37] and the Gentile Galatian believers were to think of themselves as 'children of Abraham'.[38] Ministry of the gospel to the Gentiles has brought them into God's covenant people.

Today, many years after Paul wrote his letters, Christians of whatever race or denomination should see themselves as part of a world-wide people with whom God has made a covenant through Christ and the Spirit. As Christians we are not alone; we belong to an international community whose history began, not with Jesus, but with the call of Abraham almost 4,000 years ago. Such an understanding will help us appreciate both the historical length and the ethnic breadth of the covenantal purposes of God.

[37] 1 Cor. 10:1.   [38] Gal. 3:7.

3:7–18
5. The glory of Moses and the glory of Christ

In opposing the ministry of his opponents' 'back-to-Moses' programme, Paul is soon involved in wide-ranging contrasts between old and new covenants. If the old mediated condemnation and death, the new mediates righteousness and life. The old covenant was temporary and is now abolished; the new is permanent and will continue without end. Above all the new covenant mediates the Spirit of God to our lives, transforming them into the likeness of Christ.

1. Temporary and permanent (3:7–11)

Now if the ministry that brought death, which was engraved in letters on stone, came with glory, so that the Israelites could not look steadily at the face of Moses because of its glory, fading though it was, ⁸will not the ministry of the Spirit be even more glorious? ⁹If the ministry that condemns men is glorious, how much more glorious is the ministry that brings righteousness! ¹⁰For what was glorious has no glory now in comparison with the surpassing glory. ¹¹And if what was fading away came with glory, how much greater is the glory of that which lasts!

Whenever we write the date on a letter, we follow, consciously or unconsciously, the long-established custom of dividing history into two parts – BC and AD. Surprisingly, history's mid-point is not an invention, or the discovery of a continent, or a war, but a person, Jesus Christ. All events are calculated in relationship to Christ, as coming before or after him. This remarkable practice has its beginning in passages like the one under discussion, where Paul divides history around Christ. His coming ended one *ministry* and began another.

The former *ministry* is characterized as belonging to Moses, the latter to Christ. Although both Moses and Christ are described as glorious (verses 7, 18), their glory is unequal. Now that Christ has come, Moses has no glory at all. Why does Paul, in contrasting the ministries of Moses and Christ, introduce the idea of 'glory' (which he uses sixteen times between 3:7 and 4:17)? The answer probably lies in the new situation in Corinth in which the Jewish missionaries are attempting to win the church over to the law of Moses. They may have claimed that Moses was equal, or even superior, to Christ, and that Christ was merely part of the covenant of Moses. Paul, in response, uses the 'glory' motif, teaching from Exodus 34:29–35 that Moses needed to veil his face to prevent the people from seeing its brightness. According to the apostle this was because the glory of Moses' face was *fading* and he did not wish the Israelites to see it fade (verse 13). In other words, Moses' ministry of the law was temporary; it was not an end in itself. The law of Moses pointed to an end beyond itself and that end was Christ. Elsewhere Paul wrote, 'Christ is the end of the law so that there may be righteousness for everyone who believes.'[1] By contrast with Moses, Christ's glory, as seen by Paul near Damascus (*cf.* 4:6), is permanent, infinitely greater and heavenly.

But why should the Corinthians have been attracted to the newcomers' message about Moses and the law? If for modern people the problem with Christianity is its antiquity, the problem people had then was its novelty.[2] People of those times venerated the past, believing that old ideas and customs went back to the gods. Cicero wrote that 'ancient times were closest to the gods'.[3] Doubtless these ministers pointed to Moses as a venerable figure and to their temple as an ancient institution. Moreover, the Jews were God's historic people who had, by that time, settled in many parts of the world and represented approximately a tenth of the population of the Roman Empire. The existence of numerous 'Godfearers' or Gentile onlookers in the synagogues is evidence of the attractiveness of Judaism to many pagans. It would have been easy enough for the newcomers to dismiss Paul as a self-appointed, self-recommended upstart peddling a heretical, novel version of Judaism.

---

[1] Rom. 10:4.

[2] *Cf.* R. L. Wilken, *The Christians as the Romans Saw Them* (Yale University Press, 1984), p. 122.

[3] *De Legibus*, 2.10.27.

Paul, in common with other New Testament writers, taught that Christ was the fulfilment of the covenant God made with the Jews, not a heretical departure from it. 'No matter how many promises God has made, they are "Yes" in Christ. And so through him the "Amen" is spoken by us to the glory of God' (1:20). The one and the same God who in the time of Moses' ministry made the promises has seen to their fulfilment in Christ, whom the apostles now proclaimed (1:19). Paul's reply to those who said that Christianity was a heretical sect of Judaism was to insist that there is one God, one covenant of promise and fulfilment and one covenant people who believe the word of God spoken as promise or fulfilment. For us now the Old and New Testaments bear witness respectively to promise and fulfilment, and together represent the Scriptures of God for the people of God.

The problem, apparently, was that these Christian Jews, in common with unbelieving Jews, insisted that the dispensation of Moses was still current. The newcomers (who were in some sense Christian, though to what extent we do not know) seem to have located Jesus within the Mosaic covenant and to have denied that he was the fulfilment of its promises or the goal to which it pointed. Paul's response is that, since God has made a new covenant (verse 6), Christians should not be looking back over their shoulders to the old. In this passage he employs two related modes of argument to persuade the Corinthians not to return to the old, but to remain in the new covenant.

First he compares the old covenant adversely with the new. The former *ministry* was marked by *death* (verse 7) and condemnation (verse 9), whereas the latter is marked by *the Spirit* (verse 8) and *righteousness* (verse 9). Paul's negative assessment of the earlier dispensation is in line with opinions of distinguished members of that covenant. 'They broke my covenant,' is Jeremiah's verdict on the Hebrews' behaviour after God rescued them from Egypt.[4] Moses, in the book of Deuteronomy, said, 'You are a stiff-necked people,' and 'to this day the Lord has not given you a mind that understands or eyes that see or ears that hear.'[5] Since they neither observed the laws God gave them, nor had any assurance of his forgiveness when they broke them, the commandments became, not the source of life as originally intended,[6] but a harsh 'letter' (verse 6) which condemned them and destroyed their fellowship with God.

[4] Je. 31:32.   [5] Dt. 9:6; cf. 10:16; 29:4.   [6] Dt. 5:33.

The new covenant, however, has exactly opposite effects. If the ministry of the letter kills, the ministry of the Spirit gives life (verse 6). If the old covenant issues in condemnation, the new issues in *righteousness* (verse 9), which, since it is the opposite of condemnation, must mean 'acquittal'. This meaning is confirmed in a later passage where Paul associates 'the righteousness of God' with 'God ... not counting men's sins against them' (5:18–21). According to that passage God does not count the sins of those who are 'in' the sinless one, who, in his death, was 'made ... to be sin' for them. In other words, under the new covenant, God forgives those who believe in and belong to his Son, who died for them. Moreover, God gives these people the Spirit, that is, his own personal presence to indwell and give life (verse 6) to them.

These twin blessings of *righteousness* and *the Spirit* are referred to elsewhere in the writings of Paul. In one passage he states that we are 'justified (= declared righteous) by faith', whereas in another we 'receive *the Spirit*' by 'believing what (we) heard'.[7] Both *righteousness* and *the Spirit* are received when we exercise faith in Christ. On one occasion he brings the two ideas together: 'If Christ (*i.e. the Spirit*) is in you ... your spirit is alive because of *righteousness*.'[8] Clearly it is because of *righteousness*, or acquittal, that God gives us life, a living relationship with himself, through *the Spirit*.

Paul's second argument against returning to the old covenant is that it is now superseded. If the former *ministry ... came with glory*, then the latter will be *even more glorious* (verses 8, 9, 11). However, it is not merely that one ministry is superior; it is, rather, that the lesser, temporary glory of the old did not continue, but concluded, once the greater, permanent glory of the new dispensation arrived. The glory on Moses' face was *fading* (verses 7, 11, 13), or, more accurately, had been 'abolished'.[9] In placing his 'radiance' on Moses' face, God set limits to its duration. By contrast, the *glory* of the new *ministry* is unlimited and permanent (verse 11). Now that the new has come, *what was glorious has no glory now in comparison* (verse 10).

In other words, the glory of the old has been 'deglorified' by the infinitely greater glory of the new. In itself the old covenant now has no glory. It is glorious now only in so far as its promises point to the glorious one who was to come. It is not that Paul disowns the former ministry. Had there been no promise, there could have been no

---

[7] Rom. 5:1; Gal. 3:2.   [8] Rom. 8:10.

[9] A. T. Hanson, *Jesus Christ in the Old Testament* (SPCK, 1965), pp. 25–35; *cf.* also Barrett.

fulfilment. Nevertheless the hands of God's clock have now moved from a.m. to p.m. Let the readers understand that the period of the old has passed, never to return. There can be no putting back of God's clock.

What emerges for us from Paul's teaching is that we must establish sound principles in interpreting the ministries or dispensations of God's covenant. We cannot, like Paul's opponents, think and act as if the new had not superseded the old. These persons were but the first of many within Christian history to have confused the covenants, as two examples will illustrate.

In the third century, Cyprian, bishop of Carthage, wrote of the holy communion and ministry in the New Testament in terms of Old Testament sacrifice and priesthood,[10] thus blurring the distinctive character of the new covenant. The subsequent loss of the distinctive New Testament views of the local congregation and pastoral ministry in favour of exalted views of church buildings and of ministers as sacrificing priests, views which developed in late antiquity, owe much to Cyprian's earlier teachings.

In the twentieth century the exodus story has been used by some liberation theologians to endorse Marxist class struggles in the Third World.[11] Not only does the original exodus narrative fail to support the modern exegesis, but, more significantly, that exegesis is done as if the old dispensation had not been overtaken by the new. The result has been, in some quarters, the politicization of Christianity and the loss of its essentially evangelical character.

These examples show that, if appropriate interpretive principles are not used, there are considerable consequences in the ecclesiastical and political spheres, to mention only two.

2. Open-faced before God (3:12–18)

Therefore, since we have such a hope, we are very bold. [13]*We are not like Moses, who would put a veil over his face to keep the Israelites from gazing at it while the radiance was fading away.* [14]*But their minds were made dull, for to this day the same veil remains when the old covenant is read. It has not been removed, because only in Christ is it taken away.* [15]*Even to this day when Moses is read, a veil covers their hearts.* [16]*But whenever anyone*

---

[10] Cyprian, *Epistle LXII*; cf. T. M. Lindsay, *The Church and Ministry in the Early Centuries* (Hodder and Stoughton, 1902), pp. 283ff.

[11] *E.g.* G. Gutiérrez, *A Theology of Liberation* (SCM, 1974), pp. 155ff.

turns to the Lord, the veil is taken away. [17]*Now the Lord is the Spirit, and where the Spirit of the Lord is, there is freedom.* [18]*And we, who with unveiled faces all reflect the Lord's glory, are being transformed into his likeness with ever-increasing glory, which comes from the Lord, who is the Spirit.*

a. The veil removed

What is the *hope* (verse 12) of which Paul speaks? The previous few verses as well as those that follow leave no doubt that it is the hope of *glory* which is in mind (verses 13ff.).[12] The ministry of the new covenant is glorious (verses 8–9): it imparts glory to those who receive it (verse 18). What is this glory? God is and always will be invisible to man; what he showed us at various critical points in the Bible story was his glory. When finally we come into his presence we will participate in his glory; we too will be glorified. The 'glory of God' vividly summarizes, in a phrase, all the end-time blessings God will bestow upon his people. This is the *hope* of God's people.

This passage continues to contrast the old and the new covenants, though the emphasis is now on the peoples of those covenants. The contrast focuses on the *veil* imagery drawn from the story of Moses in Exodus 34:29–35. The veil on Moses' *face* is metaphorically said to have been over the *minds* (verse 14) of the people of the old covenant. Paul is making two closely related points. On one hand he is referring to Moses' own words that the people wilfully failed to comprehend the meaning and significance of God's rescue of them from Egypt.[13] On the other, Paul is implying that, because of this, God did not let them understand the promises made under the Mosaic covenant which would be fulfilled in Christ. They did not see the glory in the old covenant which pointed to Christ. The result is that, though they sit week by week in the synagogue and hear passages from Moses, a veil of ignorance prevents them from understanding the scriptures which are being *read* (verses 14–15). Because of the veil the mere reading of the old covenant will achieve nothing. As Hughes comments: 'The same veil, the inward veil of which the outward veil was the symbol, is still keeping the hearts of the Israelites in darkness whenever they are confronted afresh, as it were, with Moses in the form of the Old Testament scriptures.'

The veil, which in Moses' day prevented the Israelites seeing in to

---

[12] *Cf.* Rom. 5:2.   [13] Dt. 29:2–4.

the glory behind it on Moses' face, now lies over their minds preventing them seeing out to the glory in the Scriptures, which they regularly hear. It is *only in Christ* (verse 14), in whom the promises made under the old covenant are fulfilled and whom the apostles proclaimed (1:19–20), that *the veil* is *removed*. Only as Jews are persuaded from the Old Testament that the Messiah is Jesus, and turn to him, is the veil taken away and the glory seen (verses 16, 18).[14]

What, then, does Paul mean by writing that the *Lord* to whom one turns *is the Spirit* (verse 17)? Does he mean that the Lord Jesus and the Spirit are one and the same person? Is he implying that there are two (Father and Lord=Spirit), not three, persons in the Godhead? The famous tripartite 'Grace' with which the letter concludes conclusively supports a trinitarian rather than a binitarian doctrine.

Paul, it seems, is seeking to make an important point in the present argument with the Jewish ministers. Moses turned to the Lord under the old covenant. But the old covenant is now ended in Christ and the Holy Spirit. The Lord of the old covenant has now more completely revealed himself as Father, Son and Holy Spirit. The Lord to whom we now turn is the Lord Jesus Christ. Had Paul merely quoted Exodus 34:34, the readers might have concluded that they could have turned to the Lord of the old covenant in terms of the keeping of the old covenant. The new ministers have apparently focused on Jesus 'in the flesh', that is, in terms of Jesus' Jewishness and as a law-keeper. But the old covenant is now ended, not by a merely Jewish Jesus, a Jesus of the flesh, but by Jesus who is glorified in heaven and who pours the Holy Spirit into the hearts of those who turn to him. *The Lord is the Spirit* is Paul's shorthand way of referring to the Lord of the old covenant as he has now more completely manifested himself in the Lord Jesus Christ and the Holy Spirit in a new and spiritual covenant.[15]

The imagery of the veil, therefore, is central in the contrast Paul is making between the people under the old and under the new covenants. Moses and the Jewish people are veiled, whereas Paul and other Christian people are *unveiled* (verse 18). W. C. van Unnik has shown that to cover the face means 'shame and mourning' whereas to

[14] *Cf.* Acts 17:2–3.
[15] Calvin comments that 'the statement before us ... has nothing to do with Christ's essence but simply points out his office'.

uncover the face means 'confidence and freedom'.[16] In other words, because of condemnation under the old covenant the people were shamefaced and hesitant in the presence of God, whereas, because of the 'righteousness' through the ministry of the new covenant, the people are open and confident with their God. Those who turn to the Lord who is the Spirit possess *the Spirit* and enjoy *freedom* (verse 17), whereas the others are, by implication, still in a state of slavery.

b. Beholding the glory

Since the veil is a metaphor for blindness it is clear that those who are under the old covenant are blind to the glory of God, whereas those under the new 'behold' (RSV) the glory, which they see in the *face*, or person, of Jesus Christ (verse 18, *cf.* 4:6). Those whose minds are veiled from the glory in the old covenant do not change or progress. They are like creatures who live in a stagnant lifeless pond. On the other hand, those who are *unveiled* see the *glory* of the Lord Jesus and are *transformed into his likeness with ever-increasing glory*.

In the passage 3:18 – 4:6 Paul refers to 'beholding the glory' and 'seeing the light'. Does he mean this in a literal or a figurative sense? Paul himself literally 'saw a light from heaven, brighter than the sun'.[17] But does he mean that somehow, at the point of conversion, we too see some kind of light perhaps in an inward or mystical sense? What the believer 'sees' is 'the light of the gospel of the glory of Christ' (4:4), which is the 'light of the knowledge of the glory of God' (4:6). The 'light' comes by the 'gospel' or the 'knowledge of God'. As the psalmist wrote, it is 'the entrance of (God's) words' which 'gives light'.[18] Paul's language, while literal for his own unique experience, is metaphorical for believers in general. It is the light of a now enlightened understanding. Gone is the darkness of blindness; in its place is the light of spiritual comprehension.

c. Transformed into his likeness

What does it mean to be *transformed into his likeness*? It is certain that we do not change so as to resemble the Lord in any physical way. A clue to Paul's meaning may be that *the Spirit* who here *transforms* us

---

[16] W. C. van Unnik, 'With Unveiled Face', *Nov. Test.* 2/3 (1964), pp. 160–161, writes that the word *bold* (*parrēsia*) is equivalent to an Aramaic word which means 'to uncover the face'.   [17] Acts 26:13; *cf.* 9:3; 22:6.   [18] Ps. 119:130.

all (verse 18) is said, elsewhere, to produce in believers the 'fruit' of 'love, joy, peace, patience, kindness, goodness, faithfulness, gentleness and self-control'.[19] It may be that Paul's metaphorical language has in mind these nine moral and spiritual attributes which are truly descriptive of the *likeness* of Jesus, and which the Spirit achieves in us.

How does this character transformation take place? It occurs *when anyone turns to the Lord* (verse 16), so that the *veil is taken away* and we begin to 'behold' the glory of the Lord (verse 18, RSV). Although the verb can mean *reflect* (NIV), 'behold' is to be preferred because a parallel passage (4:18) uses the synonym 'look'. By this Paul means coming within the ministry of God's word, the gospel, which affirms that Jesus Christ is the image of God and also Lord (4:2–6). Through this ministry the knowledge of God is imparted to us (4:1, 6). We must take steps to place ourselves under the ministry of the gospel through church membership and also by personal Bible reading and prayer. In another letter Paul expresses the same essential idea in these words: 'Be transformed by the renewing of your mind.'[20] Clearly the process of transformation, while 'spiritual', is not mystical but educational in character. The content of the education is the gospel of Christ.

Beholding *the glory of the Lord* is to be the unchanging activity of the Christian life from beginning to end. This results in our transformation *from glory to glory* (NASB). At the beginning, the believer 'sees' the glory with his mind as he understands the gospel and turns to the Lord. At the end, he sees that glory with his eyes as, face to face, he sees the heavenly Lord, enveloped in glory. In between the beginning and ending he 'beholds' the glory through the pastoral ministry of the gospel in the church.

This passage should be read alongside Romans 8:29–30 which refers to God's great plan, stretching from eternity to eternity, by which we are 'predestined', ... justified, ... glorified'. God's purposes for us who believe overarch not only the extremities of our own lives but also of world history. The plan of God which culminates in our glorification was formed in eternity before the believer was born or the world was made. It is vital that day by day we live within this conceptual framework so that in everything we do or think we promote the growth of Christlikeness (or glorification) within our lives.

[19] Gal. 5:22–23.   [20] Rom. 12:2.

The gospel of Christ not only illuminates our darkened lives; equally remarkably, it transforms them little by little so that they increasingly resemble the moral and spiritual character of the Lord Jesus. The old covenant, by contrast, brought only condemnation and death. Paul's words *with ever-increasing glory* are triumphant. This is not, however, the missionary triumphalism of Paul's opponents,[21] or the triumphalism of the 'church militant' seen in soaring cathedrals, mass rallies or burgeoning ecclesiastical institutions. It is the triumph of the grace and power of God reproducing through the Spirit the beauty of Christ in lives which are outwardly decaying and disintegrating through their connection with the world which is 'passing away'.[22] Only the grace of God is kind enough and the power of God strong enough to achieve this transformation in our broken and darkened lives.

[21] 2 Cor. 10:13–18; *cf.* 2:14.   [22] 1 Cor. 7:31.

4:1–6
6. The face of Jesus

The bitter conflict in Corinth between Paul and his opponents now comes into clearer focus. Earlier he referred to them as the 'many' who 'peddle the word of God for profit' and as 'some' who have brought 'letters of recommendation' to the Corinthians (2:17; 3:1). Now we discover the nature of the criticisms they have made against him.

Although Paul was deeply hurt by these accusations, he does not abandon his ministry or his ties with the Corinthians, as a lesser person may have done. Many people crumble in the face of adversity. For Paul, however, the new situation appears to have stirred him to greater efforts; the letter itself is evidence of that.

In his defence Paul claims to have executed his ministry with utmost care. He has in no way altered the Christian message (to make it say what he wants it to say) or manipulated his hearers (to make them do what he wants them to do). He, the faithful messenger of God, has accurately passed on the word of God while respecting the integrity of the hearers.

1. This ministry: its method (4:1–4)

Therefore, since through God's mercy we have this ministry, we do not lose heart. [2]Rather, we have renounced secret and shameful ways; we do not use deception, nor do we distort the word of God. On the contrary, by setting forth the truth plainly we commend ourselves to every man's conscience in the sight of God. [3]And even if our gospel is veiled, it is veiled to those who are perishing. [4]The god of this age has blinded the minds of unbelievers, so that they cannot see the light of the gospel of the glory of Christ, who is the image of God.

a. This ministry

What Paul has from God, he pointedly tells the Corinthians, is *this ministry* (verse 1). His newly arrived critics, by implication, have 'that' ministry – a continuation of the ministry of Moses which issues in condemnation and death (3: 7, 9), a covenant which is now 'deglorified' by the infinitely greater glory of the new covenant which has overtaken it (3:9–11).

This ministry is, by contrast, a ministry of righteousness (3:9), of reconciliation (5:18) and of the Spirit (3:8). By means of the ministry of the new covenant the people now have boldness in the presence of God (3:12), and freedom through the Spirit both to turn to the Lord and also to be transformed into his moral and spiritual likeness (3:17–18). The excellence of 'this ministry' is the reason for and basis of his unblemished lifestyle as a minister, which he now outlines.

What Paul writes is a reply to as many as five accusations which his opponents in Corinth have levelled against him.

(i) His *we do not lose heart* (verse 1) suggests that his opponents had accused him of having become demoralized and apathetic in the ministry. Had he not quit Corinth and then Ephesus? Was there not talk of his depressed state of mind? After all, those who had recently come to Corinth were carrying all before them, and Paul was nowhere to be seen.

(ii) The claim to have *renounced secret and shameful ways* (verse 2) likewise indicates that the newcomers were claiming that Paul was guilty of such things. In other words they were saying that he was a dishonest and devious man.

(iii) His reply, *we do not use deception* (verse 2), refers to their specific charge that he declined the Corinthians' financial support in order to have some subtle bargaining power over them. He refers to this again when he writes, 'I have not been a burden to you. Yet, crafty fellow that I am, I caught you by trickery!' (12:16).

(iv) Similarly, his *nor do we distort the word of God* (verse 2) implies an accusation of having added to or diluted the message about Christ. This may refer to Paul's teachings about 'righteousness' and the 'Spirit' (3:8–9) which his Judaizing opponents would regard as heretical additions to their gospel. Paul made the counter-charge that they 'peddled God's word' (2:17) and proclaimed another Jesus and a different gospel (11:14). Clearly this was a battle over true doctrine.

(v) Finally, it appears that they accused him of obscuring the gospel, doubtless from law-conscious Jews who could not make sense of Paul's Messiah-centred message which treated the Mosaic law as outmoded. In writing *even if our gospel is veiled* (verse 3) he is, to a degree, conceding their point against him. Paul knew from bitter experience how few Jews accepted his message. The veiled mind which hindered their apprehension of the glory to which the old covenant pointed (3:14–15; *cf.* 1:9) also prevented their receiving the apostle's proclamation of its fulfilment in the Son of God.

How does Paul respond to these accusations?

(i) Against the charge of being demoralized and having given up, the apostle writes as 'having' (present tense) *this ministry* (verse 1) as indicative of his ongoing commitment. The unscheduled visit to Corinth, followed by one letter, then another, with a further visit pending, are all clear evidence that Paul has by no means given up either the ministry or the Corinthians. It is not that he persevered because of inborn 'true grit' but rather it is because 'this ministry' imparts forgiveness, the Spirit and the glory of God. The effects of ministry are reason enough for continuing with it.

The need for perseverance in ministry is not confined to stipendiary ministers. The New Testament is clear that every believer is given gifts by God with a view to ministry.[1] Times of discouragement come to everyone engaged in ministry, with the accompanying temptation to give up. Whatever our ministry may be, we do well to say with Paul: *Since ... we have this ministry, we do not lose heart.*

(ii) and *(iii)* As to the generalized accusation of being secretive and devious, and, more specifically, his crafty motives for declining their support, he declares that he is *setting forth the truth plainly* (verse 2). His opponents have placed him in a very difficult position. He cannot leave their criticisms unanswered, but when he makes a reply they complain that he is 'commending himself'. While it is clear that they too engage in self-commendation (10:18), it is also clear that Paul's commendation is different. 'The distinction between Paul's self-commendation and that of his rivals', writes Barrett, 'is that he acts *in the sight of God*. And he appeals to the *conscience*.'

What does Paul mean by *setting forth the truth plainly*? The words, literally, are 'by the manifestation of the truth', the truth, that is, of

[1] 1 Cor. 12:7; Eph. 4:7; 1 Pet. 4:10.

the *word of God* (verse 2). He makes no claim to innate goodness or to personal adequacy. Indeed, he has already referred to having been 'under great pressure, far beyond our ability to endure, so that we despaired even of life itself' (1:8). His answer to those who criticize him is that the word of God is the basis of his life, so that all that he does expresses and manifests that word. In other words, despite his personal problems, which he does not hide, he is living sincerely as a Christian and commends himself as such to the consciences of others. Moreover, he does this in *the sight of God* (verse 2; *cf.* 2:17; 12:19). Paul has the deep conviction that God witnesses all his motives and actions (1:23), and that everything he has done will be apparent on the day of judgment (5:10).[2] These two facts – that the word of God is the basis of life and that God is witness and judge of all we do and think – have the potential powerfully to effect the behaviour, not only of Paul, but of all other Christians as well.

(iv) Paul is adamant that he did not *distort the word of God* (verse 2). Although he is referring to the spoken as opposed to the written word, it is obvious that both Paul and the Judaizers regarded the gospel as having a specific content. The problem was that they had sharply differing opinions of that content so that both accused the other of adding extra elements and therefore of diluting the true message (2:17; 4:2; 11:4). What were the elements in Paul's gospel which his critics regarded as extraneous? While there is no way of being certain, we may reasonably suppose that the doctrines which are prominent in this letter, and for which he argues, may well have been under dispute with his critics in Corinth. In essence 'the word of God' is that Jesus Christ, God's Son, is Lord. That 'word' says it all, so that to add to it really subtracts from Christ, the source of its power.

The elements in Paul's gospel which would have caused acute difficulties for Jews, including many Jewish Christians, were those which emphasized that the covenant of God with Israel was now fulfilled or ended (3:13).[3] In particular, his proclamation of Jesus Christ as the 'Son of God', the 'Yes' to all the 'promises of God' (1:19), must have created grave problems for the members of that race. Similarly his insistence that the new covenant had superseded a deglorified covenant which issued only in 'condemnation' and 'death' (3:7–9) could not fail to have provoked a strong reaction in those loyal to Moses and the law.

[2] *Cf.* 1 Cor. 4:5.   [3] *Cf.* Rom. 10:4.

The focus of these assertions which so gravely affected Jews was, of course, Jesus Christ. Presumably the Christian Jews who opposed Paul would have concentrated on the human Jesus as a faithful member of the Jewish people and as one who taught and interpreted the law of Moses. It is quite possible that the pre-Christian Saul of Tarsus may well have been untroubled by such inoffensive doctrines. As a Christian, however, Paul emphasized the heavenly Lord who had been crucified – Jesus as the Son of God, the Lord, and the image of God, the 'glory of God in the face of Christ', and the 'one who died for all', who was 'made to be sin'.[4]

It was not merely a case of one set of theological opinions in conflict with another – Paul's against the Judaizers. Twenty years earlier Paul would have shared the presuppositions of those who now opposed him. It was the Damascus Road event, the circumstances of which are so strongly embedded in this passage,[5] which radically altered Paul's way of thinking about Jesus and therefore of Judaism. On that fateful day, the moment the glorious heavenly figure identified himself as Jesus, Paul's whole frame of reference began to change. So far from being 'under God's curse' because he was 'hung on a tree',[6] as he had previously believed, Paul now understood that Jesus was actually sent by God to bear the curse of God on sin as an atonement for mankind (5:14–16).

So many of the distinctive references to Jesus in this letter, which spell the end of the old covenant, are directly traceable to the Damascus Road event – the 'Son of God', the 'Lord', 'light', 'glory', and the 'Spirit'.[7] The contents of Paul's gospel, therefore, were not different from the newcomers' as a matter of opinion only, but as a matter of history – God's revelation of his Son to Saul of Tarsus near Damascus in the year *c.* AD 34. Paul's theology, as stated in this letter, arose out of the Damascus Road event.

(*v*) While accepting that for many Jews in particular his gospel message *is veiled*, Paul by no means agrees that this is due to a content which is defective or diluted. Furthermore, there is nothing in Paul's behaviour which obscures the word of God. He attributes the veiling to *the god of this age*, Satan, who has *blinded the minds of unbelievers, so that they cannot see the light of the gospel of the glory of*

---

[4] 2 Cor. 1:19; 3:16; 4:4–6; 5:14, 21.
[5] See S. Kim, *The Origin of Paul's Gospel* (Eerdmans, 1981), pp. 3–31.
[6] Dt. 21:23.
[7] Gal. 1:14; Acts 9:3, 5, 17; 22:6, 8; 26:13, 15.

THE FACE OF JESUS

Christ (verse 4). The blindness of man to the word of God is due not to any human agency but to the activity of Satan.

b. The god of this age

The sinister figure of the devil is portrayed as *the god of this age* (verse 4). The RSV translates 'world', not 'age', suggesting the idea of place, as if the devil were god over the planet earth or the universe. But the original word *aiōn* (English 'aeon') really means an era of time, an epoch. The NIV translation 'age' has much to be said for it. In similar passages we note that Jesus spoke of 'the cares of the age' while Paul wrote of 'this present evil age'.[8] Thus the Bible is not being negative about the physical world; on the contrary, what God created he called 'good ... very good'.[9] From the biblical perspective it is the *age* commenced by Adam's rebellion, not the created world, which is evil. The creation is merely the stage on which the tragedy of man's sin is enacted. The Scriptures teach, however, that the revolt against God began not with man but with Satan.[10] Humanity has, in reality, been caught up in the cosmic and supernatural uprising of Satan against the one true and living God. Thus mankind is said to be the 'children of the devil' or of 'the evil one'.[11] John wrote that the 'whole world lies in the evil one',[12] the imagery suggesting that the human race lies helpless in the coils of a huge serpent. The evil one is also said to be 'in the world',[13] that is, inhabiting and controlling the minds of all people everywhere. Hughes comments that 'the unregenerate serve Satan as though he were their God'.

By what means does the evil one control the world? He *has blinded the minds of unbelievers* (verse 4). While the emotions and the will are unquestionably involved in our response to God, he first of all addresses our minds. It is with the mind that, metaphorically speaking, we *see the light of the gospel* (verse 4) and *the light of the knowledge of the glory of God* (verse 6).

The Achilles' heel of man is his mind, since he is so prone to intellectual pride, especially in matters to do with religion.[14] It was with unerring judgment about human vulnerability, therefore, that Satan *blinded*, not the emotions, or the will, but the *mind* of man.

[8] Mk. 4:19 and Gal. 1:4 in Greek.
[9] Gn. 1:4, 10, 31.
[10] 1 Jn. 3:8.   [11] 1 Jn. 3:10, 12.   [12] 1 Jn. 5:19, my translation.
[13] 1 Jn. 4:4.   [14] Rom. 1:21–25; *cf.* 1 Cor. 1:21; 8:1–2.

2. This ministry: its content and effect (4:5-6)

For we ho not preach ourselves, but Jesus Christ as Lord, and ourselves as your servants for Jesus' sake. [6]*For God, who said, 'Let light shine out of darkness,' made his light shine in our hearts to give us the light of the knowledge of the glory of God in the face of Christ.*

a. Preaching

How did Paul exercise 'this ministry'? What was its characteristic activity? The 'ministry' is expressed by preaching (verse 5). It is regrettable that the distinctive activity of the apostle has such negative associations today. The very word evokes images of religious buildings, strangely dressed clergy and long, dull sermons. 'Preaching' certainly sounds off-putting to modern people. But what did Paul mean by 'preach'? In his day the word we translate as 'preach' was not primarily a religious but a secular word.[15] The verb *keryssein* comes from the noun *keryx*, meaning a 'herald', a person who brought important announcements from a king or emperor to his people, scattered throughout his kingdom. An approximate modern equivalent to the ancient *keryx* is the radio or television news reader who announces the news to the listening world. Like the modern news broadcaster the ancient 'herald' had to possess a good speaking voice and the self-discipline not to embellish or alter the message. It is unfortunate that the profound and good news of God about Jesus Christ has been made to appear trivial and narrowly religious by associations with the word 'preaching'.

b. Jesus as Lord

What is the content of Paul's preaching? It may be important that Paul first states that *we do not preach ourselves* (verse 5) and concludes the sentence by saying *ourselves as your servants* (literally, 'slaves'). This is directed at the new ministers who claim to be superior to Paul (11:5) and whose ministry 'enslaves' the Corinthians (11:20). Their preaching, apparently, focused on themselves and had the effect of making the Corinthians serve them. These persons have the dubious distinction of being among the first of many subsequent

[15] Except that the secular society of that period was also very religious and the *keryx* often proclaimed information from the king that was religious in character. See *TDNT* III, pp. 688-694, 698-700.

ministers who, in the name of Jesus, have placed the spotlight on themselves in order to achieve some psychological or material benefit from their followers. By constrast, the apostle preaches *Jesus Christ as Lord* (verse 5). Paul's words here vividly recollect the Damascus Road event. The *Lord* whom he preaches was spoken of in verse 4 as the 'glorious' image of God whose *face*, in the following verse, is said to radiate *the glory of God* (verse 6). Paul referred to this in the earlier letter when he wrote: 'Last of all he appeared to me also'.[16] Although in that passage Paul lists himself with those to whom the risen Lord appeared, he is probably speaking of the glorified heavenly Jesus as he is and will be, eschatologically, rather than as he was. Thus he spoke of himself as 'abnormally born', that is, as privileged, prematurely, to see Christ in his end-time glory. Paul was determined to present Christ to others with no glory subtracted through personal self-promotion. Paradoxically the message of the glorious Lord is effectively conveyed only by those who have the mind and manner of a servant. Calvin commented: 'He that would preach Christ alone must of necessity forget himself.'

c. Glory

2 Corinthians 3:7 – 4:6, 16–18 is dominated by the theme of *glory* (*doxa*), about which J. Jervell[17] helpfully comments: 'The divine *doxa* is in the way God exists and acts, that is God himself. If the *doxa* of Christ is mentioned, that means that God himself is present in Christ.' Since God has glorified Jesus, Jesus must belong to God and be the climax of God's great saving acts in history. It was the *glory of God in the face of Christ* (verse 6) which above all changed the direction of the life of Saul of Tarsus. Paul knew immediately it was God himself who in his *glory* had confronted him in the glorified Jesus. Hence Jesus Christ whose *face* (or 'person'; Greek *prosōpon*, verse 6) Paul saw is described as the *image* of God (verse 4). Moreover the 'glory of Christ' (verse 4) is one and the same thing as the *glory of God* (which is *in the face of Jesus Christ*, verse 6). This close identification between God and Jesus will perhaps account for the great emphasis Paul places on Jesus as the Son of God (1:19).[18] Barrett writes that 'in God's Son God himself is encountered, yet at the same time remains the Invisible One'.

---

[16] 1 Cor. 15:8.   [17] J. Jervell, *Imago Dei* (1960), quoted in Barrett.
[18] See M. Hengel, *The Son of God* (SCM Press, 1976).

d. Gospel light

The Damascus Road event, upon which Paul depends so strongly for his view of Jesus, is also important as a description of Christian conversion. The bright glory Paul saw with his eyes near Damascus is now also said to be internalized in the *hearts* of all who hear and believe the preaching about the glorified Lord. Once again Paul establishes a close identification between the God whom he had known as a Jew and the Lord Jesus whom he now knew. It is one and the same God who at creation said, '*Let light shine out of darkness*' who now shines his *light* in the *hearts* of believers by means of the gospel (verse 4), which is *the knowledge of ... God* (verse 6).

At the beginning of the creation, when all was darkness and chaos, 'God said, "Let there be light," and there was light.'[19] God now addresses his gospel word to sinful people whose lives are, metaphorically speaking, darkness and chaos. As we hear and submit to his word, God shines his light into our hearts, dispelling the darkness of ignorance, guilt and fear. It is a new creation (5:17), of which we are now part, achieved by the word of God.

The 'god of this age' who 'has blinded the minds of unbelievers' (verse 4) is, therefore, limited in his power; he is not omnipotent. God has placed in the hands of his people the more powerful instrument of the gospel which can actually overcome this blindness and allow the light of God to break into human hearts. This is the point at which we particularly observe the sovereign power of God the creator. Satan, the petty tyrant, is capable only of removing sight; God actually restores sight, through the gospel, so that the spiritually blind can see.

Are we intimidated by the aggressive opposition of non-Christians? Do we feel helpless in the face of the 'god of this age'? We should reflect on the powerful gospel God has placed in our mouths. By means of this message, ordinary people, as 'God's fellow-workers' (6:1), are able to convey the light of God into human hearts and bring about a new creation. In the exercise of what he calls 'this ministry' the apostle is an example for all subsequent Christians as one who humbly and unceasingly proclaimed that Jesus Christ is Lord.

[19] Gn. 1:1, 3.

4:7–18
7. Eternal glory

In what he now writes Paul touches on some of the harsh realities of human existence – suffering and physical decay (4:7–18), death (5:1–9) and judgment (5:10–21). These are universal realities no-one can evade, which is perhaps the reason that this part of the letter has struck such deep responses in Paul's readers.

But in consistently writing *we ... our*, is not Paul speaking about his own suffering and death, not those of people in general? While he is referring to himself (and his apostolic circle) in 4:8–15 it seems he moves beyond that in 4:16 – 5:10 to make universal statements. Comments about his personal difficulties and death (verses 8–12) refer back to the 'sentence of death' (1:8–10) he believed himself to be under. These have apparently stimulated Paul to make theological statements about the destiny of all believers.

It is interesting to ask why Paul should have raised these matters immediately after the section in which he declared the old covenant to be outmoded, overtaken by the new. One possible answer is that because the apostle himself had so recently stared death in the face he could not help writing about it. Another is that for all their words about power, the new ministers in Corinth have nothing to say about suffering, death and judgment. Ultimately they are concerned with transient and superficial matters. But in the new covenant of righteousness and the Spirit, God meets humans in their suffering, death and judgment – at their points of deepest need.

1. Power in weakness (4:7)

But we have this treasure in jars of clay to show that this all-surpassing power is from God and not from us.

Paul contrasts a priceless jewel with its receptacle, an everyday earthen jar. The jewel, or *treasure*, is 'the knowledge ... of God in the face of Christ' which God has 'made ... shine in our hearts' (verse 6). The earthen jar in which this treasure is contained, the human body, is subject to decay and vulnerable to disease and injury. It is, in ultimate terms, powerless.

This is not accidental, but deliberate, *to show that this all-surpassing power is from God* (verse 7). The power to lift man out of his powerlessness in the face of suffering, decay and death does not come from within himself; it comes only from God. Man is like a *jar of clay* in order that the *all-surpassing power* might be from God, and not from ourselves. Earlier (1:8), he wrote of being 'under great pressure, far beyond our ability to endure'. Now, in exact answer, he writes of God's power which surpasses the weakness of the human body.

It is, apparently, part of God's plan that the power is *not from us*. Had this priceless treasure been contained in a strong and permanent body it would have proved a fatal combination for proud and sinful man. Like Adam, he would have reached for the heavens to be a spiritual superman, a 'god',[1] a reference perhaps to Paul's opponents (*cf.* 12:6–7, 11). We come to appreciate how powerful God is only when we acknowledge the certainty of our own death. This, apparently, had been Paul's experience. Human life is short, its form easily defaced and its fabric destructible in a second. It is an earthen jar, a cheap clay pot. Hughes comments that 'the immense discrepancy between the treasure and the vessel serves simply to attest that human weakness presents no barrier to the purposes of God, indeed, that God's power is made perfect in weakness'.

This teaching about power in weakness, so far from being applicable only to the apostles, is, along with the teaching on transformation (3:18) and illumination (4:6), true for all believers. In fact, the opinion that the power of God impinges on man not in his supposed strength but in his real weakness is no passing sentiment, but is the theological insight, the chief theme, which binds together the whole letter and gives it its unity. It was stated near the beginning (1:8), is restated here (verse 7) and will reappear near the end in the memorable words of Jesus to Paul: 'My power is made perfect in weakness' (12:9).

---

[1] Gn. 3:5.

2. Deliverance (4:8–9)

We are hard pressed on every side, but not crushed; perplexed, but not in despair, [9]*persecuted, but not abandoned; struck down, but not destroyed.*

The intruding ministers in Corinth apparently spoke of power and triumph in the Christian life. Down the centuries many have eagerly listened to impressive-sounding preachers who have raised the hopes of their hearers that they too, like the speaker, can enter new and high levels of religious experience. Some who embrace these hopes so much want them to be true that they feel unable to admit to any problem or even a 'down' mood. Paul, however, is emotionally honest. He does not cover up his difficulties, but, as one conscious of being a 'jar of clay', reveals something of his sufferings and hardships. In speaking of being *hard pressed* he is referring to those pressures' which impinge on him because he is a Christian. Being *perplexed* means a feeling of being 'cornered'. He says he is *persecuted* or 'hounded', doubtless on account of his ministry. Finally, he confesses to being *struck down*, which probably means, in our language, 'depressed'.

While most of these problems arose from his particular calling, many will recognize and identify with his feelings. Most readers know, to some degree, what he means by these things. Ordinary people will be encouraged to know that their difficulties were also shared by the great apostle. Yet along with each of these problems mentioned in verses 8 and 9 he adds *but not*. 'Pressured' *but not crushed*; 'distressed' *but not in despair*; 'hounded' *but not abandoned*; 'depressed' *but not destroyed*. If the fourfold difficulties show that he is 'a jar of clay', the fourfold *but not* is evidence that the 'all-surpassing power is from God' (verse 7).

It seems probable that in each of the four seemingly hopeless situations Paul had prayed to God for help (see 1:8–9). He identified his problem in prayer to God. Then as the answer from God became apparent he could say *but not* .... The fourfold *but not* encourages us to pray specifically about our own personal areas of distress and difficulty. According to Hughes, Paul is 'speaking the language of experience ... – the experience simultaneously of his own incapacity and of God's transcending power which transforms every situation'.

3. Death in us (4:10–12)

We always carry around in our body the death of Jesus, so that the life of Jesus may also be revealed in our body. [11]*For we who are alive are always being given over to death for Jesus' sake, so that his life may be revealed in our mortal body.* [12]*So then, death is at work in us, but life is at work in you.*

The *death* (better, 'dying') *of Jesus* which Paul carries *around in his body* (verse 10) refers back to the fourfold distress of verses 8–9 and anticipates the two longer lists of suffering in 6:3–10 and 11:23–29. Examination of the three passages reveals that the *death of Jesus* in Paul's *body* is his way of speaking of the physical and emotional pain associated with his ministry of the new covenant. Examples of physical pain are stated briefly in the second list as 'beatings' and 'imprisonments' (6:5), with much greater detail given in the third list. Emotional suffering includes, from the second list, 'dishonour', 'bad report', being 'regarded as imposters' (6:8), and from the third, 'concern for all the churches' (11:28). It may be that Paul believed his death process was actually accelerated in the pursuit of apostolic ministry.

While Paul is referring primarily to himself and his apostolic associates, what he writes will apply to other Christians who give themselves in ministry in a world environment which is generally unsympathetic. A Christian employee is passed over for promotion or is dismissed because he or she is a godly person who will not bend the rules. A missionary doctor loses her place in the structures of the profession because she has spent ten years in an out-of-the-way hospital. A pastor and his family pass up the security of their own home in obeying the call of God to serve, now here, now there. While there are great compensations, all ministry is costly not only in terms of what one relinquishes to pursue it but also in the accompanying misunderstanding or abuse, perhaps from friends and family. This cost, whatever it means in specific circumstances, is part of what Paul means by carrying *around in* the *body the death of Jesus* (verse 10).

There is a close connection between *death … at work* in Paul and *life* in the Corinthians (verse 12). The apostolic labours and teaching of Paul, which meant that his own life was being forfeited, were the means by which the *life* of God, through the Spirit, was *at work* within them. Without Paul's 'death' there would be no 'life' for the Corinthians. This principle of life arising out of death or costly sacrifice originates with Jesus. Jesus' death, literally speaking, is the *source* of eternal life to humanity; the death of those who minister, metaphorically speaking, is the *means* of life for mankind.

But what does Paul mean by *so that the life of Jesus may also be revealed in our body* (verses 10–11)? By 'the life of Jesus' he means, first, the four 'but nots' of verses 8 and 9. That the Christian does not succumb to his problems and difficulties is evidence that *the life of Jesus* is *revealed* within him, through the transcendent, sovereign power of God. Paul, however, is also speaking of the future when God's resurrection power will finally deliver us from death (see verse 14). Then, too, *the life of Jesus* will be manifested within us, but permanently.

4. Motives for ministry (4:13–15)

It is written: 'I believed; therefore I have spoken.' With that same spirit of faith we also believe and therefore speak, [14]because we know that the one who raised the Lord Jesus from the dead will also raise us with Jesus and will bring us with you in his presence. [15]All this is for your benefit, so that the grace that is reaching more and more people may cause thanksgiving to overflow to the glory of God.

Having stated that 'death is at work' in him so that life may be at work in the Corinthians, Paul now proceeds to state two reasons or motives for his sacrificial lifestyle.

The first is that he has *that same spirit of faith* (verse 13) as the writer of Psalm 116 who thankfully testified to God's deliverance of him from death. Paul's recent and profound awareness of death (1:8–10) had led to an intensified understanding of the 'all-surpassing power' of God to deliver him (verse 7). In particular, his more deeply realized faith that *the one who raised the Lord Jesus from the dead will also raise us* (verse 14) has led the apostle to say with the psalmist *we also believe and therefore speak* (verse 13). So far from having lost heart (verses 1, 16), as his critics claim, the recent experience of deliverance from death has strengthened Paul's resurrection faith, and because of this he writes, *we ... speak* (the Greek implies 'continue to speak') the word of God.

The second reason for his missionary zeal was his passion for *the glory of God* (verse 15). Paul laboured in the ministry of the new covenant so *that more and more people* (verse 15) would come to understand the *grace* of God and *cause thanksgiving to overflow* to him. Paul longed that men and women who 'neither glorified (God) as

God nor gave thanks to him'[2] would, in increasing number, be converted through the gospel and express thankfulness to God, and so glorify him.

This passage is an interesting example of the way Paul introduces important doctrines in an incidental way. His focus is on two reasons for involvement in evangelism – the eschatological (God *will raise us*) and the doxological (*thanksgiving, to the glory of God*). To make his point he tells us, in passing, that God has raised Jesus from the dead and that others whom God will raise will be brought into the presence of Jesus, presumably for judgment (see 5:10). Since what Paul says about resurrection is introduced so inconspicuously, we are the more confident to regard the resurrection of Jesus as historically true.

5. Eternal glory (4:16–18)

Therefore we do not lose heart. Though outwardly we are wasting away, yet inwardly we are being renewed day by day. [17]*For our light and momentary troubles are achieving for us an eternal glory that far outweighs them all.* [18]*So we fix our eyes not on what is seen, but on what is unseen. For what is seen is temporary, but what is unseen is eternal.*

a. Perseverance

We do not lose heart, he declares (verse 16), repeating the exclamation of verse 1. In the former reference it was the knowledge of what God was doing *through* him that kept Paul at his task, despite opposition and discouragement. By means of 'this ministry' he was imparting life to the dying and sight to the blind (3:6; 4:6). Yet the cost to him in the pursuit of the 'ministry' of the new covenant was, apparently, the acceleration of his own death process (verse 12). Now, in verse 16, his perseverance as an apostle flows out of this understanding of what God is doing *in* him.

b. Outwardly and inwardly

While Paul wrote verses 8–15 from the viewpoint of an apostle, with only indirect application to believers in general, he penned verses 16–18 as an apostle and a Christian and so they apply directly

[2] Rom. 1:21.

to all Christians. While Paul suffered and felt the power of death within as he exercised his ministry, he also knew that all people, in fact, suffer and are conscious of their mortality. Therefore what is happening to him (verses 16–18) is happening to all; in writing *we ... our* he writes for all.

The distinction between *outwardly* and *inwardly* must be carefully understood. Paul is not distinguishing, as the Greeks did, body from soul or body from mind, but rather is considering our 'total existence from two different view points' (Harris). By *outwardly* Paul means a person in 'his creaturely mortality' (*ibid.*), as belonging to this age, which 'is passing away'.[3] By *inwardly we* Paul means the person who belongs to the age to come, who already possesses the Spirit of the new age. According to Barrett, Paul is employing 'the peculiar Christian eschatology, which insists that the age to come has already (but not completely) come into the present'.

For many the awareness of aging and physical decline is accompanied by anxiety and depression. Denney observed that 'the decay of the outward man in the Godless is a melancholy spectacle, for it is the decay of everything'. Perhaps Paul was untouched by such fears? Apparently not, for how else can we explain his insights into suffering and death unless he felt these deeply? Why does Paul not *lose heart*? It is because God will raise his body from the dead (verse 14). More, he knows that the progressive decay of himself outwardly is being accompanied by the proportional renewal of himself inwardly. Calvin wrote that 'it is necessary that the condition of the present life should decay in order that the inward man may be in a flourishing state'.

While it is not too difficult to know what Paul intends us to understand by *outwardly we are wasting away*, the meaning of *inwardly we are being renewed day by day* (verse 16) is not self-evident. It can be said, however, that he does not mean only that our inner lives are renewed day by day in the sense of being repaired or refreshed. It is more particularly that God is creating within our inner nature a new person out of the old, so that when it is finished it will be completely new. It is by faith, not sight (5:7), however, that we understand that *inwardly we are being renewed day by day*'. The renewal of which he speaks is not something we see, feel or experience; it is apprehended by faith and hope. The problem of knowing precisely what he means by *inwardly we are being renewed* is

[3] 1 Cor. 7:31.

intensified by his shift from psychological imagery ('ourselves inwardly') to architectural imagery (building, house, dwelling) in the following verses. What these complex word-pictures appear to be saying is that God is preparing a permanent home for us after the dissolution of our present bodily frame.

c. Glory

It is helpful to notice the form of these verses. In verse 16 Paul writes of *outwardly ... wasting away* and *inwardly ... being renewed*, thus establishing a pattern of negative/positive contrasts, which he will follow in the ensuing verses. Moreover, as we examine the negative elements in the verses we discover that they are inter-related. The same is true of the positive elements; they too are connected. Thus our 'outward' selves (verse 16) belong to the present world of *what is seen* (verse 18) and is *wasting away* (verse 16) on account of *troubles* (verse 17). By contrast an *eternal glory that far outweighs them all* (verse 17) is the culmination of *inwardly ... being renewed day by day* (verse 16) which belongs to the new creation which is, as yet, *unseen* (verse 18).

What is *glory*? Man cannot see God;[4] what God shows man and permits him to see is his 'glory' or 'brightness'. God displays his 'glory' for all to see in the sun by day and the moon and stars by night.[5] He revealed his glory to his servant Moses[6] and in his Son's miracles[7] and through his death.[8] Three disciples, together with Moses and Elijah who reappeared for the occasion, witnessed the glorified Jesus on the mount of transfiguration.[9] Paul saw the glory of God in the face of Christ on the road approaching Damascus.[10]

Although 'glory' belongs to God alone, he imparts his glory to his people. Through the gospel God shines his light into the darkness of our hearts (4:6). Thereafter the Spirit progressively intensifies the glory within the believer's life (3:18). This is indeed difficult to comprehend, since our eyes tell us of decay outwardly and our consciences remind us of sin inwardly. Calvin wrote that 'the decay is visible, and the renovation is invisible'. We infer from this passage that as the decaying human frame approaches disintegration, the finishing touches are being applied to the new creation. At death the scaffolding and hession of our outer frame will be removed

---

[4] Jn. 1:18.   [5] Ps. 19:1.   [6] Ex. 33:18 – 34:8.
[7] Jn. 2:11.   [8] Jn. 12:23–24.   [9] Mk. 9:2–8.   [10] Acts 9:3–5.

and God will unveil to us the building from God, the house not built by human hands, eternal in heaven (5:1).

Earlier Paul employed the Greek word *hyperbolē* to convey the extent of his problem: 'we were under great pressure', the last word meaning 'weighed down'. Here Paul takes up the word *weight* (*baros*) and also *hyperbolē*, which he uses twice for absolute emphasis, applying it not to suffering but to glory (*cf.* RSV, 'an eternal weight of glory beyond all comparison'). In a brilliant and paradoxical statement Paul contrasts the *light and momentary troubles* of this existence with the *eternal glory* of the new creation, which *far outweighs them all* (verse 17). Seen in true perspective, the *troubles* of our outer nature are 'light' in weight and of *momentary* duration, while the *glory* of our inner nature is of heavy 'weight' and *eternal* duration. 'This comparison', Calvin observed, 'makes that light which previously seemed heavy, and makes that brief and momentary which seemed of boundless duration.' He continued, 'When we have once raised our minds heavenwards a thousand years begin to look to us to be like a moment.'

According to Paul, our *troubles are achieving for us the glory* of which he writes. It is not that he viewed sufferings as 'good works' or as virtuous in themselves. They do not automatically or mechanically intensify the 'glory'. Rather, it is that *troubles* cause us to *fix our eyes not on what is seen, but on what is unseen* (verse 18). *Troubles* help us to understand that there is no future for us here in this tawdry, fading existence. Therefore we focus, increasingly, on the unseen, resurrected and glorified Christ (4:4–6, 14). Bodily needs are important, certainly; and so are the needs of others. Yet what we are to long for is not the pleasures and possessions put before us by the advertising agencies in the media, but the promises of the gospel in the Bible. The Christian's study of holy Scripture, both privately and in the context of fellowship, prayer, worship and service, will be very important to rivet his attention on *what is unseen*.

When rust begins to appear in my car I know the time has come to think about getting a new one. The old is finished; the new is needed, sooner or later. When the signs of age begin to appear in my body I know that it is, in principle, finished; it is only a matter of time. It belongs to a world-system which is creaking and groaning with age, awaiting its renewal.[11] Physical exercise and a sensible diet are very important in a proper treatment of our bodies, which

[11] Rom. 8:21; 1 Cor. 7:31.

are a trust from God. The skill of the surgeons in transplanting organs gives hope of greater life-expectancy to many people. Nevertheless, the power of death within us is in the end irresistible. I have no power either within myself or outside by which my life can be renewed or extended in any ultimate sense; my one hope is God and the new 'dwelling' (5:2) he will give me. While this is good news it is also very humbling. If we were spiritual supermen, as the newly arrived ministers in Corinth apparently claimed to be (11:5; 12:6, 11), we would continue to believe the delusion that our future lay with this body in this world. When the signs of decay appear, as they will, we are thrown back on God and the hope of the building (5:1) which he is preparing for us.

Because *what is unseen is eternal* it is more real than the things which are seen. Our future *eternal* exsistence with God is a true existence; this one is only a shadow cast by the coming reality. By illustration, consider the Australian cicada, a large, flying insect, which makes its annual, noisy, appearance in midsummer. During its life cycle there is an outer husk, the exoskeleton, which lies underground and within which the cicada is formed over many years. At the right time the exoskeleton reaches its end and the beautiful insect flies away in freedom. The outer frame existed for the formation of that which was its true purpose, the new life which would issue from it. This life, with its *troubles*, is a preparation for our true destiny – an *eternal glory that far outweighs them all*.

d. The God who prepares

God graciously prepares for our future in a twofold way. Using our *troubles*, he prepares *for us* (verse 17) an *eternal glory*, 'an eternal house in heaven, not built by human hands' – the new habitation which will be ours at death (5:1–2). Secondly, in case we may not be spiritually or emotionally ready, God prepares us for the new existence so that we are able to receive it (5:5). God's preparation for our future is complete, being both objective and subjective: he prepares it for us and us for it.

5:1–10
8. Death and judgment

The process of dying, just described, now reaches its end in death. It may seem that this age, which is passing away, has claimed yet another victim. Death is a futility, calling into question everything a person has done, hoped for or suffered. Funerals are sad and often bewildering occasions, especially for those who do not enjoy the Christian hope.

Far from being romantic and glamourizing death, as believers sometimes do, Paul is realistic and sober. Just as the process of wasting away is a harsh reality of our existence, so too is the end of the process, the destruction of the 'earthly tent'. The effect of Paul's dark realism about dying and death, however, is to show up the contrasting brightness of the all-surpassing power of God. For just as the power of God is at work within dying man, so too the power of God is present in its fullness at his death.

Underlying Paul's exposition throughout 4:16 – 5:10 is the subdivision of history into the present and future ages. Although Paul moves quickly from one image to another, the 'two ages' frame of reference is implicit throughout. In the previous few sentences he spoke of a believer's life as 'inward' (belonging to the coming age) and 'outward' (belonging to the present age). Both aspects are subject to the forces which characterize their respective ages – outwardly we waste away through 'troubles' and inwardly we are re-created through the Spirit. In the ensuing passage (5:1–9) he writes not of our existence as inward and outward but of a total mode of human existence in this age which gives way to another total mode of existence in the coming age.

Although it has been suggested[1] that Paul's belief in the believers' corporate resurrection at the return of Christ, as expressed in 1 Corinthians 15:12–57, gives way in this passage to the individual Christian's immortality at death, close examination of both texts show this not to be the case. First, Paul has already confessed belief in the general resurrection in 2 Corinthians. A few verses earlier than the passage under review, he wrote that God will 'raise us with Jesus and will bring us with you into his presence' (4:14; cf. 1:9–10). Paul's commitment to the resurrection of believers, as a coming historical event, is undiminished in 2 Corinthians. Secondly, we find a number of key words relating to the 'present/new age' frame of reference both in 1 Corinthians 15:35–54 and in 2 Corinthians 5:1–9. In both passages we find the word 'unclothed', 'earthly' as contrasted with 'heavenly' existence, and the mortality and death of the present age being, respectively, 'clothed' and 'swallowed up'.[2] The recurrent use of these words, carrying similar meanings in both letters, is evidence that Paul's teaching on the Christian hope is unchanged.

What must be understood is that Paul was grappling with different problems in the respective passages. In 1 Corinthians Paul wrote within the framework of the present and the coming ages, the changeover point being the 'last trumpet' heralding Christ's coming and the resurrection of the dead.[3] In response to Corinthian questions and objections Paul gave examples from nature to show the reasonableness of a human existence which continued from this age to the next but which is different in outward form and appearance.

In the second letter he writes representatively of all believers who face the prospect of death before the intervention of the new age. If, in his former letter, the emphasis was 'we shall all be changed',[4] in the second letter it is 'If the earthly tent … is destroyed, we have a building from God, an eternal house in heaven' (5:1). In this letter, therefore, Paul is affirming that death in no way deprives the believer of the glory of the coming age.

---

[1] For discussion see G. E. Ladd, *A Theology of the New Testament* (Eerdmans, Grand Rapids, 1975), pp. 550–557.

[2] Cf. 1 Cor. 15:37 ('just a seed' = literally 'the bare kernel', RSV) and 2 Cor. 5:3; 1 Cor. 15:40 and 2 Cor. 5:1–2; 1 Cor. 15:53–54 and 2 Cor. 5:4.

[3] 1 Cor. 15:52–53, 42.   [4] 1 Cor. 15:51.

1. Image 1: a new, permanent dwelling (5:1)

Now we know that if the earthly tent we live in is destroyed, we have a building from God, an eternal house in heaven, not built by human hands.

It is not necessary to think, as some scholars do, that Paul now believed he would die before the Lord's coming. We note that the Christian's death is here stated conditionally (*if*) not absolutely ('when'). In the apostle's mind the return of the Lord may well precede his death. The emphasis of the verse is, rather, to contrast the inferior, impermanent, present mode of existence (literally 'our earthly tent-house') with the superior, permanent mode of our coming existence (*a building from God, an eternal house in heaven*).

The likening of death to the dismantling of a tent is understandable, given that the apostle was an itinerant leather-worker who, among other things, made and repaired tents.[5] Human life is indeed like a 'tent', being both temporary and vulnerable. The new dwelling, however, is *eternal* and *from God* (verse 1). That it is *not built by human hands* suggests that we are to think of it as a temple. Jesus used these words to describe the temple of his risen body.[6] Significantly, when one *house* is pulled down we have another, though different, *house*; death does not mean homelessness. The tent-house will be succeeded by the heavenly house. There will be continuity between this mode of life and the next. Harris[7] suggests that the force of *we have* (present tense) means immediacy of possession of the new once the old is finished. The loss of the one is followed directly by the ownership of the other, superior, dwelling.

To our minds this present existence is solid and real, whereas our coming existence seems shadowy and insubstantial. Paul teaches us that the reverse is true. The life which is to come is strong, permanent and real; the present life is lived among the shadows.

2. Image 2: a desire to be 'overcoated' (5:2–5)

Meanwhile we groan, longing to be clothed with our heavenly dwelling, ³because when we are clothed, we will not be found naked. ⁴For while we are in this tent, we groan and are burdened, because we do not wish to be unclothed but to be clothed with our heavenly dwelling, so that what is mortal may be swallowed up by life. ⁵Now it is God who has made us for this very purpose and has given us the Spirit as a deposit, guaranteeing what is to come.

[5] Acts 18:3; *cf.* 2 Pet. 1:13.   [6] Jn. 2:21; Mk. 14:58.
[7] For helpful discussion of the entire passage see M. J. Harris, '2 Corinthians 5:1–10: Watershed in Paul's Eschatology', *Tyndale Bulletin* 22 (1971), pp. 32–57.

Paul now changes his imagery from buildings to clothes. He retains for a moment a reference to a *dwelling* with which we shall be *clothed* (verse 2), thus briefly mixing his metaphors before employing the consistent and sustained imagery of a person changing his clothes. This illustration, drawn from daily life, is marked by an unusual feature.

Normal practice is to remove the clothes we are wearing before we put on the new ones. In Paul's imagery, however, he writes of putting the second set of clothes *over* the first without removing them. What he wishes to avoid, if possible, is that period between the two sets of clothes when we would be *unclothed*.

What does he mean by his illustration? The two sets of clothing represent, respectively, our existence in the present and in the coming age. In the present age *we groan and are burdened* (literally 'we sigh, deeply burdened', verse 4). This is not an expression of dissatisfaction with our present existence, a yearning for death to bring to an end this present life (*we do not wish to be unclothed*, verse 4). Rather it is the profound longing to be 'overcoated' with all the blessings God has for us in the new age.

Nevertheless, he makes the point, in passing, that even if we are *unclothed*, that is, if our death precedes Christ's return, *we will not be found naked* (verse 3). This refers, apparently, to his teaching on baptismal commitment: 'All of you who were baptized into Christ have been clothed with Christ.'[8] Paul's desire to avoid being unclothed arose from a human shrinking from the experience of death before the parousia rather than from a sense of guilt before the all-seeing eye of God. His understanding that on becoming a Christian believer he had 'been clothed with Christ' delivered him from the fear of being 'naked' before the all-seeing eye of God.

Paul introduces, briefly, a further image to reinforce his point. He desires that his *mortal* existence will not merely stop, but, before it ends, *may be swallowed up by life* (verse 4). Paul depicts the new age (*life*) as, let us say, a larger fish overtaking and swallowing whole a smaller fish (his mortality in this present age).

Our longing for the *life* of the new age does not arise from within us. Left to ourselves we may not be happy with our new home or our new clothes; they may not be what we expected. It is God who has graciously prepared us for all that his great future holds (verse 5).

By *the Spirit*, who belongs to the new age, but whom God has

---

[8] Gal. 3:27 where *endysasthai* approximates to the *ependysasthai* of 2 Cor. 5:2, 4.

given us now, we are being prepared for our new dwelling, our new apparel. The presence of the Spirit within us is signified by the deep longing believers experience for their future with God. Our 'sighing' for it is inspired by the Spirit, who, however, is not yet present in his fullness; that is reserved for the coming age. What we have now is the Spirit as a *deposit, guaranteeing* an expected future payment in full. A 'guarantee' (*cf.* 1:22) was used in Paul's time in commercial transactions; today the same Greek word is used for an engagement ring, pledging and guaranteeing the marriage day.

3.   Image 3: a preference to be at home with the Lord (5:6–9)

Therefore we are always confident and know that as long as we are at home in the body we are away from the Lord. [7]*We live by faith, not by sight.* [8]*We are confident, I say, and would prefer to be away from the body and at home with the Lord.* [9]*So we make it our goal to please him, whether we are at home in the body or away from it.*

Paul's third main image for the two modes of existence in the present and coming age related to home life. It is based on the simple truth that a person can be in only one place at a time. He is either *at home in the body* (verse 6) or *at home with the Lord* (verse 8). His preference is to be *away from the body* because this will mean being *at home with the Lord* (verse 8). This 'at/away from' imagery, however, is not coldly geographical but warmly relational, as indicated by the words *with the Lord*. In a number of other places in the New Testament the preposition *with* (*pros*) is used of people being in relationship with one another. For example, the people of Nazareth ask, in response to Jesus' presence with them: 'Isn't this the carpenter? Isn't this Mary's son and the brother of James, Joses, Judas and Simon? Aren't his sisters here *with* (*pros*) us?'[9]

Although the coming age is present with us now in the 'downpayment of the Spirit' (verse 5), given to us by God, our life in the present is to be marked *by faith not by sight* (verse 7). In the new age we shall 'see' and be *with the Lord*, but in the present age we relate to him *by faith* exercised in response to the gospel. This is a sober corrective to enthusiastic Christians like the Corinthians who, in desiring spectacular and miraculous signs,[10] were demanding from God in the present time what really belongs to the future. A firm, well-balanced hope for the future is clearly encouraged in

[9] Mk. 6: 3; *cf.* Jn 1:1–2.   [10] See 1 Cor. 14:12; *cf.* 1:7; 13:1–2; 2 Cor. 12:12.

Scripture; a heightened eschatology with its unrealistic expectations, being ultimately destructive to faith and witness, is not.

In writing of the great prospect of being *with the Lord*, Paul does not allow us to lose touch with our present existence *at home in the body* (verse 6), in regard to which he twice affirms *we are always confident* (verses 6, 8). Certainty about the future enables believers to be courageous in the present in the face of conflict and pain. In the present existence, moreover, *we make it our goal to please* (verse 9) the Lord before whose *judgment seat we must all appear* (verse 10). He is not to be thought of, however, as a severe judge bent on condemning his servants. They are his friends, saved by him, destined to live for ever with him (verses 6, 8). Just as a child seeks to please a kindly and encouraging teacher, so we seek to please the Lord in all we do. Hope for the future, therefore, should not encourage dreamy unpracticality in the present, but courage and purpose.

4. Unanswered questions

Paul's exposition of the future age in these verses leaves a number of questions unanswered. If death precedes the coming of the Lord, is the believer 'asleep'[11] or 'with the Lord'? Is the deceased Christian in the grave, awaiting the 'last trumpet', or is he in heaven? Unfortunately Paul does not systematically set out a timetable of personal eschatology, either in this passage or elsewhere in his writings. Any attempt to piece together coherent answers to these questions will be incomplete, and to a degree, speculative. With those provisos, however, we may state that the believer is said to be with the Lord both in the coming of the Lord[12] and also when, at death, he 'departs' to be 'with Christ'.[13] From his viewpoint the present age ends and the future age commences either when he dies or at the 'last trumpet', whichever comes first.

It is difficult, therefore, to avoid holding some theory of what is called the 'intermediate state' of existence between death and the general resurrection. For Paul, death meant 'gain' which he explains as 'to depart and be with Christ'. The passage under review suggests the immediate possession of 'a building from God' when the 'tent' is destroyed (verse 1). To be *away from the body* is to be *at home*, at once, *with the Lord* (verse 8).

[11] 1 Thes. 4:14, 17.   [12] 1 Cor. 15:23.   [13] Phil. 1:21-23.

We have no information about the bodily form of the believer between his death and the resurrection of the body. The effect of what Paul writes, however, is to encourage a deep sense of security about our future even if we are unable to develop a detailed description of the 'intermediate state'. On the one hand Paul assures the Colossians that their 'life is hid with Christ in God' and that 'when Christ ... appears' they 'will appear with him in glory'.[14] As a hymn-writer interprets it:

> So nigh, so very nigh to God,
> I cannot nearer be;
> For in the person of his Son
> I am as near as he.[15]

On the other hand the apostle, following the Lord,[16] refers to believers as 'asleep'. Deceased Christians only appear to be dead. For our comfort let them be regarded as 'asleep', secure in God's keeping, to be awakened and reunited with living believers at the coming of Christ.[17]

5. Understanding power in weakness

Strong and paradoxical contrasts mark the whole passage 4:7 – 5:9. The apostle had written of treasure in jars of clay (4:7), of death and life (4:12), of outwardly wasting away and inwardly being renewed (4:16), of light and momentary troubles and eternal glory that far outweighs them all (4:17). Now he speaks of an earthly tent and a building from God (5:1), of being unclothed and clothed (5:4), of being at home in the body and away from the body (5:6, 8) and of being away from the Lord and at home with the Lord (5:6, 8).

It is quite possible that Paul is using these contrasts to correct the false teaching of the newcomers. Their preoccupation with such visible, tangible things as Israel, the temple, the law and circumcision might well be designated as 'fixing their eyes on what is seen' (cf. 4:18), or 'living by sight' (cf. 5:7). Hope for them, apparently, was limited to the religious and political systems of the here and now.

While Paul was committed to a practical expression of Christianity, as for example in the collection of money for the needs of

---

[14] Col. 3:3. [15] C. Paget, 'A mind at "perfect peace" with God'.
[16] Jn. 11:11. [17] 1 Thes. 4:14–15.

Christians elsewhere (see chapters 8 – 9) he knew that here-and-now solutions, important as they may be, do not deal with the ultimate realities of death and judgment. The Jewish Jesus of a Mosaic covenant as proclaimed by the newcomers could give no comfort to dying, sinful man, to man in his weakness. While, for them, the power of God was displayed in 'what is seen', in bigness and success, for Paul the power of God is unleashed in our weakness. As we waste away outwardly we are re-created inwardly, by the Spirit, for the new age. At the point where our tent-body is dismantled, we have another, better, permanent, glorious body – a building from God, eternal in heaven.

6. The judgment seat (5:10)

For we must all appear before the judgment seat of Christ, that each one may receive what is due to him for the things done while in the body, whether good or bad.

In Roman cities the governor sat on the judgment seat to hear court cases. Indeed, Paul had earlier stood before the judgment seat of Gallio in Corinth[18] just as the Lord stood before the judgment seat of Pilate.[19] The time is coming, however, when Paul and everyone, Pilate and Gallio included, must *appear* or be 'made manifest' (RV) *before the judgment seat of Christ*, where every secret will be brought to light.[20] For Paul, who knows that he has a new 'building from God' the moment he dies (verse 1), it is not therefore condemnation that he fears (for there is none in Christ)[21] but evaluation. It is not the loss of salvation – which cannot be lost – but the loss of commendation which is at stake. Such an understanding is completely in line with the Lord's teaching on the accountability of a steward to his master with respect to the faithful use of gifts entrusted to him.[22] God's gift to Paul was to be an apostle; the gospel was entrusted to him.[23] One day he would stand before the Lord to give an account of his faithfulness as a missionary. Whatever our ministry from God, it is sobering to note that what each one of us has done will one day be made manifest at the judgment seat of Christ.

How faithfully have we used our time? How well have we pursued opportunities? How single-minded have we been in our Christian

---

[18] Acts 18:12.   [19] Mt. 27:19.   [20] 1 Cor. 4:5.   [21] Rom. 8:1.
[22] Lk. 12:42–48.   [23] 1 Cor. 9:17.

service? The teaching about the judgment seat before which all must come, believers included, reminds us that we have been saved, not for a life of aimlessness or indifference, but for a life of serving the Lord. The balanced view, of which the prospect of the Lord's judgment seat reminds us, is that while we are justified by faith alone, the faith that justifies is expressed by love and obedience.[24] We are saved not *by* good works but *for* good works.[25] One day each of us will stand before the judgment seat of the Lord and all that we are and have been will be visible. Paul took this very seriously, for he immediately writes, 'Since then, we know what it is to fear the Lord, we try to persuade men.' A healthy fear of the judgment is a true motive in every believer as he serves the Lord in the gospel.

[24] Gal. 5:6; Rom. 1:5.   [25] Eph. 2:8, 10.

5:11–21
9. The ministry of reconciliation

The passage following is the most comprehensive statement about the death of Christ made by the apostle Paul. There are two closely related reasons for this, both connected to the challenge of the intruding ministers to the gospel taught by him to the Corinthians. First, the apostle has shown how the new covenant of Christ and the Spirit is God's powerful provision for man in his most profound experience of weakness. Having written at some length about dying and death, he now shows how the new covenant provides for the third element in the grim triad, alienation from God due to sin (5:16–21). As such these words belong to and are the climax of the whole section on apostolic ministry (2:14 – 7:1), the reference to 'ministry of reconciliation' (verse 18; cf. 6:3) clearly pointing back to and depending on the earlier words 'ministers of a new covenant' (3:6).

Secondly, since the new ministers have disparaged the ministry of Paul, he is at pains to remind the Corinthians of both what he teaches and the manner in which he conducts himself (6:1–13). This passage, therefore, is deeply personal and with many autobiographical allusions, all rooted in his experience of the Damascus Road event when he became 'in Christ' (verse 17). 'From now on' (verse 16) he lived for the one who had loved him (verse 14) and died and risen again for him (verse 15). Hatred for Christ, as Paul's controlling motive, had now been replaced by the overwhelming sense of Christ's love for him. He no longer regarded Christ in purely superficial terms (verse 16), as the crucified and therefore the accursed one, but as the one in whom God had been present to reconcile the world to himself. Moreover, in that decisive moment near Damascus, God gave the now enlightened Paul the ministry (verse 18) and message (verse 19) of reconciliation, whereupon he constantly sought to persuade people (verse 11) to be reconciled to God (verse 20). Let the Corinthians understand that what this man teaches is not merely one opinion among others but the outworking of his historic encounter with the risen Christ on the road to Damascus.

1. Paul's ministry: a basis for pride (5:11–13)

Since then, we know what it is to fear the Lord, we try to persuade men. What we are is plain to God, and I hope it is also plain to your conscience. [12]*We are not trying to commend ourselves to you again, but are giving you an opportunity to take pride in us, so that you can answer those who take pride in what is seen rather than in what is in the heart.* [13]*If we are out of our mind, it is for the sake of God; if we are in our right mind, it is for you.*

Paul's allusion to *those who take pride* (verse 12) brings the newcomers into focus once more.[1] In what do they take pride? It is *in what is seen*, their position (literally 'face', *prosōpon*, verse 12), which Paul explains as being *out of* their *mind* (verse 13),[2] a reference to their ecstatic behaviour. It seems that the new ministers were seeking recognition on the basis of bizarre religious trances or gibberish, doubtless as a sign of their inspiration by God.

Paul's admission *if we are out of our mind* (verse 13) is written to anticipate a possible rejoinder from the Corinthians that Paul also was in this condition. Did he not 'speak in tongues more than all' of them?[3] Surely Paul too, by his tongues-speaking, was trying to legitimize his ministry by means of position or 'appearance' – the very thing he complains the newcomers are doing. Paul's reply is that his glossolalia is something private; it is *for God* alone, presumably as an expression of personal devotion. It is not done to support his apostolic claims.

For you, however, he tells the Corinthians, *we are in our right mind* (or 'self-controlled', verse 13). Käsemann comments that 'the realm of private religious life ... is marked off from the realm of apostolic service to the community, which is described ... as being of sound mind'.[4]

---

[1] Refer back to 'so many, who peddle God's word' (2:17) and 'Do we need, like some people, letters of recommendation?' (3:1).
[2] *Cf.* Mk. 3:21.   [3] 1 Cor. 14:18.   [4] Quoted in Barrett.

Nevertheless the Corinthians need to be able to say something in defence of Paul. It would be helpful if there were some quality or achievement about which they might express confidence in him. The *opportunity* (verse 12) for which they should *take pride in* Paul, he tells them, is that he *persuades men* (verse 11),[5] that is, he engages in evangelism (verse 20). It is the 'ministry' therefore, and his faithfulness of it, which are to be the basis of Corinthian confidence in Paul. This source of pride in Paul is not something esoteric or bizarre; his ministry, being public, *is plain* to the Corinthians' *conscience* just as Paul himself is *plain to God* (verse 11). Mystic experience or ecstatic behaviour in ministers, therefore, should play no part in their recognition or accreditation, though such things may validly belong to their private world of relationship with God. What matters is that the would-be minister is active in 'persuading' others to become Christians and that he does so in a 'self-controlled' way in the public exercise of his ministry.

If the object of 'persuading men' was to be 'reconciled to God' (verse 20), his motive for doing so was the *fear* of *the Lord* (verse 11), the fear, as the previous verse stated, that 'we must all appear before the judgment seat of Christ'. To stand before the Lord Christ seated on his throne of judgment is indeed a fearful thing, but for whom – Paul or the people he sought to persuade? It is quite probable that he was thinking of the judgment of both sinners and the servants of the Lord. Paul knew that his ministry as an apostle would be subject to judgment with the giving or withholding of commendation as the outcome.[6] He also knew that sinners, 'objects of wrath',[7] face the just condemnation of God if they do not accept reconciliation with God through Christ. Whether, therefore, Paul thought of the sinners' or the servants' judgment, the fear of the Lord inspired him to *persuade men*. While fear is not the highest motive for behaviour, it is, nevertheless, a valid motive. Fire and heat are realities that can injure or kill; we treat them with great respect. That 'we must all appear before the judgment seat of Christ' is also an objective reality. It is one which motivates us to exercise our ministries so that on the one hand we are commended and, on the other, those to whom we speak are not condemned.

Paul is confident that he has been faithful in his apostolic ministry. Furnish comments that 'Paul's ... apostolate is validated

[5] An indication of the integrity of the Acts account of Paul's ministry may be seen in the many references to his 'persuading' others: Acts 17:4; 18:4; 19:8, 26; 26:28; 28:23–24.

[6] 1 Cor. 4:1–5; *cf.* 3:15.   [7] Eph. 2:3.

by nothing else but the congregation's own experience of having been established and nurtured by its preaching and its pastoral care'. By these few words, therefore, Paul gently reminds the Corinthians of his work as an evangelist and pastor so that they may indeed be proud of him and have something to say to his detractors.

2. The scope of ministry: all people (5:14–15)

For Christ's love compels us, because we are convinced that one died for all, ana therefore all died. [15]*And he died for all, that those who live should no longer live for themselves but for him who died for them and was raised again.*

a. The love of Christ

Paul has mentioned that two legitimizing characteristics of his ministry are 'persuasion' and a 'right mind'. He now adds a third: in all that he does he is controlled by the *love of Christ* (verse 14). The verb *compels* (verse 14) is also used on the occasion when the people were 'crowding' Jesus.[8] The Acts employs the same verb to explain that Paul 'devoted himself exclusively to preaching' after the arrival of Silas and Timothy in Corinth.[9] In this passage Paul tells us he is so controlled by Christ's love that there is no other course of action open to him but to pursue his ministry. It is worth noting that prior to the Damascus Road event the compelling force in his life had been murderous bigotry.[10] Now love has taken the place of hate at the centre of his being.

How is it possible to be motivated by the fear of the Lord and the love of Christ? Are not fear and love irreconcilable? It all depends on a proper understanding of fear and love, which, it should be noted, are not opposites. The opposite of love is hate. In the Bible 'fear' is not cringing terror but holy reverence, and 'love' is not romantic feelings but sacrificial care. The two words are consistent and reconcilable. Indeed, the fear of the Lord and awareness of the love of Christ fit perfectly together to provide the true motivation for Christian ministry.

[8] Lk. 8:45.

[9] Acts 18:5. The use of the word is another example of the way Acts is in touch with the dynamics of Paul's ministry.

[10] Acts 9:1; *cf.* Gal. 1:13.

[11] It is clear that Christ is the one who shows rather than receives love in this passage, since it goes on to say that the one who loves died for all; Christ loved and Christ died.

b. One died for all

How did Paul know that he was the object of Christ's love? It was, he continues, *because … one died for all* (verse 14). Formerly, as a Pharisee and zealot, the crucified Jesus and his followers had been the object of Paul's hatred.[12] His words *we are convinced* (verse 14) indicate that a point was reached when he reversed his opinions. So far from viewing Christ as an object of hate because of his accursed heretic's death on a tree, Paul concluded, instead, that he, Paul, was the object of Christ's love. Christ had actually died for him. In his crucifixion, Paul now understood, Christ had *died for all*, including Paul. Why did Paul change his mind? Clearly it was the Damascus Road event, in which the despised crucified one, now enveloped in glory, spoke to the prostrate Paul. Since glory could come only from God, the glorified Jesus clearly had the stamp of divine approval. The one crucified upon the tree was indeed accursed, but, as Paul now knew, it was because he bore the curse of the punishment of sin in the place of all people. There is no power so great, no motivation as strong, as the knowledge that someone loves me. Paul's understanding that Jesus, in his death, loved *him*, was now the controlling force in the apostle's life.

The association between Christ's love and Christ's death became central in Paul's exposition of the gospel. He wrote that 'the Son of God … loved me and gave himself (= died) for me',[13] and that 'God demonstrates his own love for us in this: While we were still sinners, Christ died for us.'[14] In discussing verses 14–15 James Denney commented: 'The importance of this passage is that it connects the two relations in which Paul is in the habit of defining Christ's death, that is its relationship to the love in which it originated, and the sin with which it dealt.'[15]

Paul is able to speak of the love of Christ displayed in his death either in the staggering universal terms *one died for all* or in the deeply personal 'the Son of God … loved *me* and gave himself for *me*'. Christ's love is seen either in the immensity of the numbers loved or in the intensity of his love for each individual. The *all* for whom he died are the sum total of individuals, like Paul, whom he loved. The extent of Paul's ministry, and its intensity, both of which are set

---

[12] Acts 9:1; Gal. 1:13.
[13] Gal. 2:20.
[14] Rom. 5:8.
[15] J. Denney, *The Death of Christ* (Tyndale Press, 1960), p. 83.

forth in this letter,[16] seek to give expression to the love of Christ shown to Paul.

The universal scope of Christ's love and Christ's death is seen not only in the words *one died for all* but also in the enigmatic corollary *therefore all died* (verse 14). We can understand that *one died for all*, but what do the words *therefore all died* mean? The *all* in both parts of the sentence is clearly to emphasize the universal, inclusive nature of Christ's death; none is excluded from the sphere of God's saving purposes in Christ. Paul ministered to *all* because Christ loved all and died for all. Christ's death for *all*, however, was for the definite purpose *that those* to whom Paul spoke and who were still alive *should no longer live for themselves but for* Christ. Christ's death, in other words, was intended to procure their 'death' – their 'death', that is, to *self*-centred living. The words *therefore all died* state the universal scope of his saving death, but also give expression to the strong purpose that the death of Jesus should procure death to self. Such an understanding counteracts what Bonhoeffer called 'cheap grace', a purely passive, unmoved reaction to the death of Jesus for sinners.[17] Notice the way the words *that those who live should no longer live for themselves* are balanced by *but for him who died for them and was raised again* (verse 15). The one who receives reconciliation with God through the death of Christ now says 'No' to self and 'Yes' to Christ. There is no room for cheap grace here.

This way of explaining verses 14–15 will not please all Christians. Universalists, for instance, believe that Christ died *for all* in the sense that all will be saved automatically and that none will be condemned. Paul, however, teaches that it is 'in Christ' that we become 'the righteousness of God' (verse 21). Therefore he persuades people to be 'reconciled to God' (verse 20) and urges them 'not to receive God's grace in vain' (6:1). Reconciliation is available to all, but each must personally receive it.

'Particular redemptionists', by contrast, believe that Christ died only for the elect, and that the saving benefits of the atonement are limited to them. To hold this view it is necessary to make the words 'all' and 'world' mean significantly less then they do at face reading. Moreover, it is to ignore Paul's way of referring to the death of Christ now inclusively, now exclusively. In Romans 5:18, for example, he wrote inclusively that 'one act of righteousness was

---

[16] 2 Cor. 4:8–12; 6:1–13; 11:21 – 12:10.
[17] D. Bonhoeffer, *The Cost of Discipleship* (SCM, 1964).

justification that brings life for *all* men', whereas in verse 8 of that chapter he wrote, exclusively, 'Christ died for *us*'. We discover the same pattern within the chapter under review. Thus, on one hand, he wrote 'one died for *all*' (verse 14) and, on the other, 'God reconciled *us* to himself through Christ' (verse 18). In response to the doctrine of particular redemption we may say that although the death of Christ is sufficient for all people it is efficient only for those who believe in him. The *Book of Common Prayer* (1662) helpfully states that on the cross Jesus Christ made 'a full, perfect and sufficient sacrifice, oblation and satisfaction for the sins of the whole world'. To limit or qualify this statement is to diminish the person and the work of the Son of God.

3.   The effects of ministry: new creation (5:16–17)

So from now on we regard no-one from a worldly point of view. Though we once regarded Christ in this way, we do so no longer. [17]*Therefore, if anyone is in Christ, he is a new creation; the old has gone, the new has come!*

Twice in verses 15–16 the apostle uses the words *no longer*. This means that for the person who is now *in Christ* through the ministry of reconciliation certain things are no longer true. Such a person no longer lives for self (verse 15), no longer regards Christ from a purely *worldly point of view* (verse 16). These things which are no longer true belong to *the old* which has gone, replaced by the *new creation* (verse 17) which has now come (verse 16).

a.   *Radical reorientation*

The astronomer Copernicus, who was among the first to understand that the planet Earth was not the centre of the universe, has lent his name to what we call a 'Copernican revolution' as a description of any kind of radical rethinking. The apostle Paul is no less famous for his Damascus Road experience which changed the whole direction of his life. Even though he was an outwardly religious man, everything had revolved around him. Formerly he had lived an egocentric life as the centre of his own universe. But *now* (verse 16) this is no longer (verse 15) true. He no longer lives to and for himself; now he lives to please the one who loved him, who *died ... and was raised again* for him. Christ, not Paul, is the new centre of Paul's universe; egocentricity has given way to Christocentricity.

111

What Paul underwent through the Damascus Road event others come to as a result of the ministry of reconciliation. What ordinary believers experience is no less remarkable, since the human will is so entrenched in egocentricity, a point well made by C. S. Lewis. 'What mattered most of all', Lewis observed, 'was my deep-seated hatred of authority, my monstrous individualism and lawlessness. No word in my vocabulary expressed deeper hatred than the word "interference". But Christianity placed at the centre what then seemed to me a transcendental interferer.'[18] Lewis, like Paul, was a famous convert to Christianity and he rightly saw how profound is the change from an egocentric to a Christocentric lifestyle.

b. Radical insight

In writing *we once regarded Christ from a worldly point of view* (literally, 'according to the flesh'; verse 16) Paul is, at the same time, referring both to the newcomers and to himself. The Christ proclaimed by the intruding ministers was, apparently, entirely circumscribed within the covenant of Moses – a Jewish, law-keeping Jesus. Their high view of Moses (3:12–15) necessitated a low view of Jesus. Before the Damascus Road event Paul's knowledge of Jesus had also been 'according to the flesh', not in the sense of having known the historical Jesus, but of having a false and superficial view of him. For Paul, Jesus had been a dangerous messianic pretender whose crucifixion was proof that he was indeed the accursed of God – for the Scriptures said, 'Anyone who is hung on a tree is under God's curse.'[19]

But *from now on*, he writes, he *regarded* Christ *in this way ... no longer* (verse 16). At and since Damascus he became convinced (verse 14) that in reality 'God was in Christ reconciling the world to himself' (verse 19, NASB). It became clear, in an instant, that the glorified, crucified one could only be the Son of God who in death received God's curse; not a false Messiah, but the divinely appointed agent through whom forgiveness and reconciliation would be mediated to sinful humanity. How shallow and erroneous Paul's earlier views of Jesus were compared with the new and profound appreciation of the unique figure who alone was qualified to 'die for all'! Paul's stern opposition to the new ministers arose out of his

[18] *Surprised by Joy* (Geoffrey Bles, 1955), p.163.
[19] Dt. 21:23; Gal. 3:13.

conviction that Christianity stood or fell depending on one's view of the person and work of Jesus. False views of Jesus have been promoted throughout history, including in these present times. Such views must be as firmly opposed in our generation as they were then by Paul if the true gospel is to have its power to mediate salvation.

c. A new creation

While Paul's reference to *a new creation* (verse 17) summarizes the changes which occur within the life of any believer (*if anyone*), these changes are dramatically focused within his own life. Love was now the controlling motive (verse 14) in place of hate. Serving the one who died for him had taken the place of selfishness (verse 15). True understanding of Jesus, his identity and achievement, have replaced ignorance and error (verse 16).

The apostle's use of the vocabulary of the creation narratives of Genesis is striking. It is implied that unbelievers (as Paul had been), are blind (4:4) and live in a darkness analogous to the primal darkness of the first verses of the book of Genesis. Just as God spoke then, and there was light,[20] so too God now speaks the gospel-word and once again there is light, though it is inward within the heart (4:6). As by the agency of the word of God the world was made,[21] so now, by the word of God, the message of reconciliation, people are remade. In expressing the great and profound changes that occur in the life of *anyone* who is *in Christ* Paul not only affirms that there is a 'new covenant' (3:6), there is also a *new creation*; *the old has gone, the new has come* (verse 17).

We should note, however, what is not said about the new creation. It does not mean 'living happily ever after' or a trouble-free existence. The new creation in no way immunizes people from life's problems or pain. If in relation to humanity generally the new creation was inaugurated at the first Easter, in relation to individuals it begins with the acceptance of the message, 'Be reconciled to God.' For both mankind at large and individuals in particular the full force of the 'new creation' will not be experienced or seen until the end of history, at the return of Jesus in glory. Meanwhile, since sin and its outworkings have not yet been abolished, everyone will continue to undergo, in varying degrees,

[20] Gn. 1:3   [21] 2 Pet. 3:5.

difficulty and hardship – including those in whom the new creation has begun.

We are aware of the reality of the new creation through our new perception of Jesus and the accompanying, radical, Christ-centred lifestyle. For many people like Paul, Augustine or Luther the effect of the new creation has been dramatic, both within their own lives and also upon the people of their generation. There is also, however, an important aspect of the new creation which does not lie within our conscious experience, and which we apprehend by faith and hope. This is 'the building from God, an eternal house in heaven, not built by human hands' (5:1), which God began to construct when we began to be 'in Christ'. This process of 'edification' or 'upbuilding' continues quietly and unseen throughout our lives until, at death, when 'the earthly tent we live in' is pulled down, God presents us with a new home. When that occurs, the new creation, which to that point had been spiritual and psychological, will become physical and visible. The two aspects will be fused together in a perfect and indissoluble union.

4. The source of ministry: God was in Christ (5:18–21)

All this is from God, who reconciled us to himself through Christ and gave us the ministry of reconciliation: [19]*that God was reconciling the world to himself in Christ, not counting men's sins against them. And he has committed to us the message of reconciliation.* [20]*We are therefore Christ's ambassadors, as though God were making his appeal through us. We implore you on Christ's behalf: Be reconciled to God.* [21]*God made him who had no sin to be sin for us, so that in him we might become the righteousness of God.*

a.   'All this is from God' (5:18)

All this, writes Paul – referring to his now love-controlled life, his service of the crucified and risen Christ, his radical insight into his identity – *all this*, summed up as a new creation, *is from God*. These things, the subjective or conscious results of being reconciled to God, flow from the being of God into our hearts and minds through the word of reconciliation.

What God does in us, however, is preceded logically and historically by what God did for us through and in Christ. *God was ... in Christ* – the Son of God by whose coming the ancient promises were fulfilled (1:20), the one who though rich became poor (8:9), the one who was made sin – *God was reconciling the world to himself in Christ*. All this is *from God*.

God *gave ... the ministry of reconciliation* (verse 18) and *committed ... the message of reconciliation* (verse 19) to apostles and others he calls for this purpose. Moreover, in response to such ministry it is 'God who makes ... us ... stand firm in Christ' (1:21), 'God ... who made his light shine in our hearts'. All these things, also, are *from God* (4:6).

The whole movement towards man in his need, then, is *from God*. Certainly God works through human emotions and the circumstances of life as well as by means of human agents. Yet the initiative, the momentum and the purpose are all *from God*. The only response we can make is well summed up in the words of the doxology:

> Praise God from whom all blessings flow,
> Praise him, all creatures here below.

b. 'God ... reconciled us to himself through Christ' (5:18)

That God *reconciled us to himself* implies that we were alienated from him. But what is alienation? Alienation may be defined as the absence of trust and respect between persons. It is a word often applied to broken marriages, to industrial disputes or to antagonism between nations. Alienation implies enmity, division and the loss of communication.

In writing that God *reconciled us to himself* Paul is teaching that it is God who is the aggrieved party and that man is the cause of the alienation. The reference in context to *sins* (verse 19) and to *sin* (verse 21) make it clear that these are the source of the estrangement between man and God. It is not, however, that God counts up people's sins in a cold and legalistic way. When Isaiah told the people that

> Your iniquities have made a separation between
>   you and God,
> Your sins have hid his face from you, so that
>   he does not hear,[22]

it is plain that God's response to their sins is personal, even emotional. Similarly, early in man's history, God '*saw* how great

[22] Is. 59:2, NASB.

115

man's wickedness on earth had become ... and his heart was filled with pain.'[23] We may say that God takes man's sin personally.

Moreover, it is God who personally takes the initiative to reconcile man to himself. In the world of human alienation it is usually a third party who seeks to reconcile the alienated – a marriage counsellor where husband and wife are estranged, an impartial conciliator in the event of industrial dispute, the Secretary-General of the United Nations if there is hostility between nations. But in this case it is the wronged party, God, who initiates the action. *God ... reconciled us to himself.*

Some Christians, in attempting to formulate explanations of the atonement, have utilized analogies of an impersonal kind, such as of a set of scales with our sins on one side, outweighed by Christ's sacrifice on the other. On other occasions, Jesus' death has been referred to as an offering to placate the Father's anger at human sin. While there is some truth in these and other examples, the deeply personal character of both alienation and reconciliation, as taught here by Paul, is lost. In this passage, grammatically speaking, we have a subject, an object, an indirect object, an instrument and a verb. We should note that each element is personal. The subject and the indirect object is God, the object is fellow humans like us, and the verb 'reconcile' is personal in character. The instrument, too, is personal. So far from it being an animal or an object, it was *through Christ*, his Son, that '*God ... reconciled us to himself.*

c. 'God made him ... to be sin' (5:21)

Because we are so frequently confronted with evil, for example through the news media and television entertainment, we easily become desensitized to its abhorrent character. But God is not like that – our sin offends him, grieves him, alienates him. It cannot be otherwise. Reconciliation cannot mean the ignoring of human rebellion or the mere reducing of God's displeasure. Action was necessary; the divine disapproval must be removed. How has God done this?

God was reconciling the world to himself, the apostle writes, *not counting men's sins against them* (verse 19). While God's reconciling of man to himself is expressed in the forgiveness of which this verse speaks, there is, in fact, more that must be said. While God is

[23] Gn. 6:5–6.

merciful and forgiving by nature, he is, at the same time, the holy one who cannot simply say of evil, 'It doesn't matter; let's forgive and forget.' Because we humans are compromised by our own sins, we may say that. But God, because he is God, cannot. Therefore the statement that God does not count our sins against us is incomplete. Atonement, a means of removing sin from God's sight, is necessary as a prerequisite to forgiveness. This is why the waiting father's forgiveness of the wayward son in the famous parable[24] is only part of the gospel. What must be added is what Paul now adds, that God's reconciliation of the world to himself is made possible by the sacrifice of his Son.

The words *him who had no sin*, which come first in the Greek, evoke a great sense of mystery. They describe the Son of God (1:19), the image of God (4:4), the Lord (4:5) who was without sin.[25] And yet God *made him ... to be sin*. What does this mean? Paul had in mind that grim event, the crucifixion of Jesus. The darkened sky in the gospel story is an outward sign of the cosmic and eternal transaction which took place. Paul's words to the Galatians, in which he teaches that 'Christ redeemed us from the curse of the law by becoming a curse for us',[26] help explain his meaning here. The curse of God which falls upon law-breakers fell instead upon the accursed, crucified one, so that law-breakers can be set free. Leon Morris observed that God 'treated (Jesus) as a sinner ... made him bear the penalty of sin'.[27] Harris commented that 'so complete was the identification of the sinless Christ with the sin of the sinner, including its dire guilt and dread consequence of separation from God, that Paul could say profoundly "God made him ... to be sin for us."'

Scholars have shown considerable interest in the meaning of the word *hyper* (usually translated *for*) which occurs six times from verses 14 to 21:

'One died *for* all' (verse 14);

'He died *for* all ... him who died *for* them and was raised again' (verse 15);

'We are ambassadors *for* Christ ... we beseech you *on behalf of* Christ' (verse 20, RSV);

'God made him ... to be sin *for* us' (verse 21).

[24] Lk. 15:11–32.
[25] Jn. 8:46; Heb. 4:15; 1 Pet. 2:22; 1 Jn. 3:5.   [26] Gal. 3:13. .
[27] L. Morris, *The Cross in the New Testament* (Paternoster, 1967), p. 221.

117

Clearly *hyper* is important to help explain the significance of the death of Jesus.

Two ideas appear to be in Paul's mind in relation to Christ's death *for* (*hyper*) others – *representation* and *substitution*, though the ideas are difficult to separate. In verse 20, 'ambassadors *for* Christ' implies representation, whereas in 'we beseech you *on behalf of* Christ' the stronger idea appears to be substitution. When he states that 'One died *for* all' (verse 14) and 'he died *for* all ... died *for* them' (verse 15), since one cannot substitute oneself for many, Paul appears to envisage Christ as our representative, who, in dying and rising, achieved reconciliation with God. As an analogy we may think of David, the representative warrior, winning a great victory over Goliath for the benefit of the people.[28] Closely connected with representation is the notion of incorporation. When Christ died and rose again as our representative, we who belong to him died and rose again in him.

The other thought-model, substitution, seems to be implied in *God made him ... to be sin for us* (verse 21). The intensity of *God made him who had no sin* ... suggests that God substituted the sinless one for the sinful ones. By way of illustration Hughes points out that *hyper* was sometimes used in letter-writing where a scribe wrote in substitution for someone who was unable to write. If representation implies incorporation, then substitution implies exchange. Thus, as a result of the sinless one being made sin *for us, in him we ... become the righteousness of God*. The sinless one takes our sin in himself; the sinful ones are given the 'righteousness of God' in exchange.

Paul's vision of Christ near Damascus, whereby he discerned the glorious one to be none other than the one who had been crucified, led him to the only conclusion possible, namely that what had really taken place at Calvary was God's great act of the reconciliation of humanity to himself through Christ. The crucified one truly was the accursed of God but, as he now knew, as the sin-bearing redeemer of those cursed by God as sinners and law-breakers. Grim and awful as the crucifixion had been, it was nevertheless the great expression of God's love for man, focused in Jesus. It is for this reason, therefore, that he writes elsewhere, 'May I never boast except in the cross of our Lord Jesus Christ,'[29] words which have been echoed and re-echoed in the great passion hymns of the church. 'Love so

[28] 1 Sa. 17.
[29] Gal. 6:14.

amazing, so divine,' wrote Isaac Watts, 'demands by soul, my life, my all.'[30]

The message that Christ was crucified *for* us, therefore, draws forth from us our dependence upon him. To withhold our faith and love from him would be perverse and ungrateful. Moreover, since our sins demanded so high a price for their forgiveness, we conclude that they must be deeply offensive to God. We are left with no honourable alternative but to 'die' to sin and to live for him who, as our representative and substitute, died and was raised.

[30] The hymn 'When I survey the wondrous cross'.

5:20 – 6:10
10. Ministers of God

Reconciliation is an accomplished fact ('God ... reconciled', 5:18) and also an incomplete process ('God has committed to us the message of reconciliation', 5:19). Because the two themes overlap, it is necessary to go back to 5:20 to find the beginning of the section about the ongoing ministry of reconciliation.

1. Ambassadors for Christ (5:20 – 6:1)

We are therefore Christ's ambassadors, as though God were making his appeal through us. We implore you on Christ's behalf: Be reconciled to God. [21]*God made him who had no sin to be sin for us, so that in him we might become the righteousness of God.*

[6:1]*As God's fellow-workers we urge you not to receive God's grace in vain.*

There are two admonitions in this part of the letter: *be reconciled to God* (verse 20) and (do) *not ... receive God's grace in vain* (verse 1). To whom are these words directed? Is Paul reminding his readers of his gospel message, as he does elsewhere (*e.g.* 1:19; 4:5)? Or is he making a direct pastoral exhortation to the Corinthians? While there have been advocates of both viewpoints, it may be the case that the first admonition is a rehearsal of the apostolic gospel whereas the second is a specific challenge to the Corinthians. The first admonition is embedded in a passage which sets out Paul's message in an expansive way. The second appears to be directed to those who have already received the grace of God but who are in danger of having 'received it in vain'. Later in the letter he will warn them about giving up their 'sincere and pure devotion to Christ' (11:3). If they continue to pay attention to a watered-down message (2:17; *cf.*

4:2), then the grace of God in Christ as expressed in the true gospel will indeed have been 'in vain'. That this latter exhortation is addressed to the Corinthians is the more likely, given the direction the passage takes, concluding as it does with the unambiguously direct 'we have spoken freely to you, *Corinthians*' (verse 11). Paul's words, therefore, represent a call both to the church in Corinth and to the constituent members to return to the first principles of the gospel.

Turning now to the ministry, of which the passage speaks (verse 3), how are the Corinthians, and indeed all believers, to think of ministers of reconciliation? The apostle employs two striking word-pictures to convey what is involved in this ministry: diplomatic representative and fellow-worker.

a. *Diplomatic representative*

Who are the *we* who *are Christ's ambassadors* and who *implore* their hearers to *be reconciled to God* (verse 20)? Since, as we have seen, the whole message of 5:11ff. is strongly autobiographical, it is logical to regard the *we* as referring primarily to Paul and his apostolic associates (1:19). Nevertheless, we infer that believers in general are also involved in the ministry of reconciliation. If, as is certain, the *us* whom God reconciled to himself represents a group larger than the apostles, then the corresponding *us* to whom God gave *the ministry of reconciliation* (verse 18) must also exceed the limited number of the apostolic circle. It is, therefore, reasonable to suppose that all believers are to be caught up in the ministry of reconciliation. It may be protested that if we are not theological graduates we can hardly be expected to exercise this ministry. While a comprehensive training is important for those who engage in permanent and full-time pastoral ministry, believers in general, understanding as they do that Christ has died for them, should be able to encourage others to 'be reconciled to God'.

Although our English versions employ the noun *ambassadors*, it is in fact the verb 'to act as an ambassador or diplomat' that is used (verse 20). Since Christ is no longer physically present, Paul, and indeed all Christians, represent him and speak for him. In his death he represented (*hyper*) us; in his physical absence we represent (*hyper*) him. This means that those to whom we represent him make their judgment about him by what they observe in us. As a foreign nation

121

is judged by the behaviour of its diplomatic representatives, so non-Christians often form their opinion of Christ by the behaviour of his people. It is worth reflecting upon the fact that the means God has chosen to apply the gift of reconciliation to himself is as ordinary and human as it is. Since God makes *his appeal through us* (verse 20) it is imperative that we behave so as to bring credit to our Master.

The ministry of reconciliation cannot be exercised in a detached and cold manner. The language Paul uses is deeply emotional and passionate. 'Through us', he declares, 'God *appeals* to men and women, Christ *implores* them.' This ministry can never be performed coldly or with a 'take it or leave it' attitude.

Similarly, the hearers also need to be actively responsive to enter into a relationship of reconciliation with God. To *be reconciled to God* requires that a person ask God for the forgiveness he has provided in the death of his Son. This is clear in the teaching of Jesus where 'to be reconciled' means to seek for and receive forgiveness from the wronged party.[1] God will surely forgive; there is no doubt about it. But we must ask, and this means humbly acknowledging our need for forgiveness by God.

b.   Fellow-worker

Although the NIV uses the noun *fellow-worker*, the RSV accurately conveys the meaning by using the verbal phrase 'working together with' God (verse 1). The word *synergein* (to work with) is made up of the preposition *syn* (with) and the verb *ergein* (to work). The apostle Paul, and all Christians, represent Christ and 'work with' God. This speaks both of our very considerable privilege in acting as colleagues of God and also of the resources of divine power by which he enables us to make his appeal to others. We are not helpless and alone as Christ's representatives. God has made us partners, co-workers with himself in his great rescue mission to reconcile the world to himself.

2.   Ministers of God (6:2–10)

For he says,

> *'At the time of my favour I heard you,*
> *and on the day of salvation I helped you.'*

I tell you, now is the time of God's favour, now is the day of salvation.

[1] Mt. 5:23–24.

³*We put no stumbling block in anyone's path, so that our ministry will not be discredited.* ⁴*Rather, as servants of God we commend ourselves in every way: in great endurance; in troubles, hardships and distresses;* ⁵*in beatings, imprisonments and riots; in hard work, sleepless nights and hunger;* ⁶*in purity, understanding, patience and kindness; in the Holy Spirit and in sincere love;* ⁷*in truthful speech and in the power of God; with weapons of righteousness in the right hand and in the left;* ⁸*through glory and dishonour, bad report and good report; genuine, yet regarded as impostors;* ⁹*known, yet regarded as unknown; dying, and yet we live on; beaten, and yet not killed;* ¹⁰*sorrowful, yet always rejoicing; poor, yet making many rich; having nothing, and yet possessing everything.*

a. An urgent ministry

If Paul's exhortation 'Be reconciled to God' (5:20) is an example of his 'persuading' people in general (5:11), then his 'we urge you' (verse 1) may refer to the Corinthians in particular. Directed, so it appears, to only some of the Corinthians, this appeal is made necessary by their present uncertainty about Christ and the gospel which has been created by the newcomers. Some at least are now interested in the 'other Jesus' as proclaimed by them in a 'different gospel' (11:4). There is now the serious danger that the original response to the apostolic gospel may have been *in vain*. Thus Paul is recalling them to the true Jesus and the authentic gospel.

He introduces an element of urgency in order to prompt the erring Corinthians to mend their ways speedily. Quoting the prophet Isaiah, Paul emphasizes that *now is the time of God's favour* when God will hear them, *now is the day of salvation* when God will help them.[2] Once a person and a congregation have accepted the gospel it has become the *now*-time; the *day of salvation* has dawned. We may suppose, therefore, that Paul would have sounded this urgent note both in his initial appeal at the point of conversion as well as in his pastoral exhortation to wayward believers. The writer to the Hebrews makes a similar appeal: 'Encourage one another daily, as long as it is called Today, so that none of you may be hardened by sin's deceitfulness.'[3] Furnish writes that 'for Paul, the *day of salvation* heralded by the gospel is also a day of decision for those who are addressed by it, and the claim, as well as the gift, is renewed every day that the believers continue to live in the world'.

It is not that Paul is applying some kind of psychological pressure

[2] Is. 49:8.
[3] Heb. 3:13.

on his readers, through evangelists have sometimes been guilty of this. It is, rather, that in true evangelism God himself draws near through the words of the human spokesman. It is God who summons people to enter and remain in a relationship of reconciliation with himself. The day of salvation has dawned through the death and resurrection of Christ. Because of who it is that addresses us, and the seriousness of what he says, it is appropriate to urge upon the hearers acceptance of the offer of forgiveness while it remains open.

Moreover, since it is God himself who makes his word plain to us, we should not presume that what is comprehended today will be clear to us tomorrow. In God's purposes we are not at all times equally receptive to the truth. Therefore to the reader, whether already Christian or not yet one, we say with Paul, 'Accept reconciliation with God *now*.'

b. An honourable ministry

Earlier Paul spoke with pride about 'this ministry' (4:1) that is, the ministry of the new covenant (3:6) by which those who receive it are declared 'righteous' (3:9; 5:21) and the life-changing power of the Holy Spirit (3:8, 18) is released into their lives. In affirming that the entire process of reconciliation issues from God, he states that the ministry of reconciliation, also, is the gift of God to those who exercise it (5:18).

Paul's deep concern, therefore, is for the good name of the *ministry* (verse 3). Since 'message' and 'ministry' are so closely connected (5:18–19), Paul was determined that nothing in his life should be a *stumbling block in anyone's path, so that our*[4] *ministry will not be discredited* (verse 3). In negative terms he so lived that none could blame him for unworthy behaviour. Positively, as *servants of God* he and his companions sought to *commend* themselves *in every way* (verse 4). Paul made real efforts, therefore, to avoid behaviour which would offend, while at the same time fulfilling a lifestyle which commended himself to others as a servant of God. Commenting on this passage Hughes writes: 'Nothing is more likely to cause the name of God to be blasphemed and mocked by unbelievers than the example of a minister whose conduct of himself is evidently a contradiction of the transforming power of God in Christ which he advocates in his preaching.'

---

[4] Literally, '*the* ministry ... .

In what follows (verses 7–8), Paul appears to be answering accusations which his opponents in Corinth were now making. They accuse him of employing untruthful speech, human power and the weapons of unrighteousness. In response he claims to use *truthful speech*, the *power of God* and *weapons of righteousness* (verse 7). They say he is guilty of *dishonour* and is of *bad report*, an *imposter* and an *unknown* person. He answers that his ministry is marked by *glory* and *good report*; that he is *genuine* and that he is, in fact, well *known* (verses 8–9).

In other words Paul is claiming that his behaviour, which is scrupulously honourable, is itself evidence that he is a true minister of God's authentic message.

c. A sacrificial ministry

It seems that the newcomers in Corinth presented a triumphalist (2:14) or powerful image of ministry, as many have done to this present time. They sought commendation and recognition as ministers on the basis of ecstasy, visions, revelations and miracles and other manifestations of power. Paul, by contrast, points to experiences of weakness in the exercise of his ministry (5:13; 12:7–10). Although the Jesus whom he proclaims is the glorified heavenly Lord (4:5–6) who 'lives by God's power', the Jesus who legitimizes Paul's ministry as genuine is the one who was 'crucified in weakness' (13:4). It is therefore not power, but weakness, the weakness of the one who 'died for all', as reproduced in the lifestyle of the minister, which authenticates it as a true Christian ministry.

The list that follows contains some references from the earlier as well as the later sufferings-catalogues.[5] (The appearance of words common in each list is an argument in favour of the unity of the letter. One word is common to the first and second lists; five words are found in the second and third lists.) In this passage he refers to *great endurance* (or 'patience in adversity'), *troubles* (or 'pressures', *cf.* 4:8), *hardships* (or 'inescapable difficulties', *cf.* 12:10), *beatings* (*cf.* 11:23), *imprisonments* (*cf.* 11:23), *riots* (or 'chaotic situations'), *hard work* (or 'laborious toil', *cf.* 11:23), *sleepless nights* (due to all-night tent-making? *Cf.* 11:23) and *hunger* (*cf.* 11:27).

The apostle Paul's experience of pain in the ministry represents an extreme case. Nevertheless all faithful ministry of reconciliation will

---

[5] 2 Cor. 4:8–9; 11:23–33; 12:10.

involve, to some degree at least, a measure of suffering. It is clear that the sacrifice of Christ (5:18–21) is to beget a spirit of sacrifice among those who are engaged in the ministry of the gospel.

3. Ministry: summary

Paul has shown clearly that ministers of God can never be proud or self-serving. Sacrifice is at the heart of the gospel and also at the heart of ministry – whether it is in evangelizing unbelievers or providing pastoral care for the flock of Christ. The service of God, where it is true to him, is never easy and is frequently painful. It will be remembered that Paul wrote, earlier, 'Death is at work in us, but life is at work in you' (4:12). The 'life' which they now enjoy in their relationship with God through Christ has been at the expense of the 'dying' of Paul through whose ministry they are now reconciled to God.

6:11 – 7:4
11. Paul's appeal to the Corinthians

This passage marks the end of the 'long digression' (2:14 – 7:4), a lengthy part of the letter which has been devoted to 'ministry' – the 'ministry of the new covenant' and of 'reconciliation'. Paul concludes, appropriately, with a twofold appeal to the Corinthians – to be reconciled to him and to separate themselves from over-close involvement with 'unbelievers'.

1. Paul's appeal for reconciliation (6:11–13)

We have spoken freely to you, Corinthians, and opened wide our hearts to you. [12]*We are not withholding our affection from you, but you are withholding yours from us.* [13]*As a fair exchange – I speak as to my children – open wide your hearts also.*

Paul refers to his readers by name only when he is deeply stirred – as by the bewitchment of the Galatians (3:1), the kindness of the Philippians (4:14) or, as here, by his own expression of deep affection for the Corinthians. As the one through whom they had spiritually come to birth, Paul saw himself as their father.[1] It is as their spiritual father that he now speaks to them affectionately (verse 13).

These words are not without their pathos, coming as they do after the list of suffering involved in his ministry. Spiritually speaking, the Corinthians owed their all to the apostle. When with them in Corinth he had not spared himself to bring them to birth in Christ. In his absence and for their nurture he had written four letters.[2] The

[1] 2 Cor. 12:14; 1 Thes. 2:11; 1 Cor. 4:15.
[2] Two of them have not survived; see 1 Cor. 5:9; 2 Cor. 2:4.

two which have survived are among his longest works. He had done much good to them and no harm (7:2). As a father loves his child, so the apostle Paul loved the Corinthians.

He twice employs the perfect tense to convey that, as he first loved them, so he still loves them and he will continue to love them. His freedom in appealing to them is the manifestation of a *heart* which is *opened wide* in its affection for them. And yet – and here the pathos may be felt by us – the love which he had shown has been neither received nor reciprocated. So *wide* is the affection of the apostle that the Corinthians are present within his heart (verse 3); so narrow the heart of the Corinthians that they have almost no place for him. For the newcomers who bring a false Christ and who take advantage of the Corinthians there is a warm welcome; for the genuine apostle who loves them there is only a cramped, begrudged response. Clearly Paul expects that a warm and affectionate relationship should exist between minister and congregation. This is something that both ministers and people should seek to achieve.

Paul breaks off this personal appeal (which he resumes in 7:2) to digress about separation from paganism.

2. Paul's appeal for separation (6:14 – 7:1)

Do not be yoked together with unbelievers. For what do righteousness and wickedness have in common? Or what fellowship can light have with darkness? [15]*What harmony is there between Christ and Belial? What does a believer have in common with an unbeliever?* [16]*What agreement is there between the temple of God and idols? For we are the temple of the living God. As God has said: 'I will live with them and walk among them, and I will be their God, and they will be my people.'*

> [17]*'Therefore come out from them*
> *and be separate, says the Lord.*
> *Touch no unclean thing,*
> *and I will receive you.'*
> [18]*'I will be a Father to you,*
> *and you will be my sons and daughters,*
> *says the Lord Almighty.'*

[17:1]*Since we have these promises, dear friends, let us purify ourselves from everything that contaminates body and spirit, perfecting holiness out of reverence for God.*

Paul's teaching about the new covenant, which began in chapter 3 and which finds its conclusion in this passage, was given in response to the activities of the newly arrived Judaizers. It is probable that they regarded the apostle to the Gentiles as being at best half-hearted in his attitudes to the moral code of the old covenant and as not having upheld the agreement to 'abstain from food polluted by idols' entered into at the Jerusalem Council in the later 40s.[3] To strict Palestinian and Pharisaic Christian Jews Paul's directions to the Corinthians about food sacrificed to idols would have appeared decidely weak.[4]

Paul did not, in most circumstances, disallow the eating at home[5] of food previously offered to the idol before being sold in the shops. But he strongly opposed believers eating such food in an idol's temple.[6] So far from being soft on the Gentiles in moral matters, as his critics claimed,[7] the apostle took a very firm line on the peculiarly Gentile sins of idolatry and sexual immorality.[8] '*Flee* from sexual immorality' ... '*flee* from idolatry' he had warned the Corinthians in the first letter.[9] Paul does not wish to be misunderstood. The coming of the new covenant of Christ and the Spirit in no way permits the worship of idols or attendance at pagan temples.

Paul's sensitivity to criticism from the Jewish Christian quarter on this matter was, perhaps, intensified by a failure of Gentile believers in Corinth to make a clean break with temple worship. It is possible, in fact, that there had been some recent lapsing back into pagan worship. 'Many', he wrote later, '... have not repented of the impurity, sexual sin and debauchery' (12:21).

If Athens was a city 'full of idols',[10] so too was Corinth. A century later in his description of Corinth, Pausanias mentions, in addition to the temples of Apollo and Aphrodite, some twenty images 'in the open', six other temples of the Greek gods and five precincts for the 'Lords' of the mysteries.[11] Corinth was, in Paul's words, a city of 'many "gods" and many "lords"'.[12] Small dining rooms accommodating a dozen or so people formed part of these temple complexes. It was customary for hosts to invite friends to a meal in the name of a god. Prayers to the god would then occur during the banquet.[13]

---

[3] Acts 15:20.   [4] 1 Cor. 10:23 – 11:1.   [5] 1 Cor. 10:25–30.
[6] 1 Cor. 8:10; 10:14–22. See further G. D. Fee, 'II Corinthians VI.14 – VII.1 and Food Offered to Idols', *NTS* 23 (1977), pp. 140–161.
[7] Rom. 3:8.   [8] 1 Cor. 10:6–8.   [9] 1 Cor. 6:18; 10:14.   [10] Acts 17:16.
[11] *Description of Greece*, Book II, 2–5 (Loeb edition, pp. 253–273).
[12] 1 Cor. 8:5.
[13] See further G. H. R. Horsley, *New Documents Illustrating Early Christianity* (Macquarie University Press, 1981), pp. 5–9.

Study of this passage and of corresponding sections in the first letter make it clear that Paul called on the Corinthians not to attend these temples or to participate in the meals held there.

This passage may have originally been a mini-sermon,[14] which Paul now incorporates within the letter. It is possible to think of it as an opening exhortation, a rhetorical expansion, underlying Old Testament 'promises', and a concluding exhortation.

The opening exhortation *Do not be yoked together with unbelievers* (verse 14) is the key to the whole section. All that follows relates back to this negative demand. It is a simple metaphor based on Deuteronomy 22:10, which forbade the yoking of ox and ass together, suggesting that 'the Christian is a different breed from the unbeliever and is forbidden an improper relationship with him'.[15] There is no call here, as is often claimed, for Christian to separate from Christian for doctrinal or ethical reasons. Neither is Paul requiring a wholesale separation from unbelievers. If a Christian is married to an unbeliever the believer should not seek divorce.[16] If invited to the home of an unbeliever he is free to attend.[17] Unbelievers were not forbidden to attend the Christian meetings.[18] Indeed, as Paul writes earlier, total separation from the immoral, the greedy, the robbers, the idolators would necessitate going 'out of the world' altogether.[19] Rather, as the rhetorical expansion which follows makes clear, it is a specific and technical association with temple worship which the apostle forbids. For this reason it is doubtful that Paul would agree with Christians today attending inter-faith services with Muslims or Hindus, for example, since that would mean being mismated with unbelievers.

Five rhetorical questions, set out in balanced pairs, and each requiring a negative reply, are now asked. The point of each question is that God's people are to be distinct and separate from the characteristic beliefs and practices of unbelievers. Thus there is nothing *in common* between *righteousness and wickedness*, no *fellowship* between *light* and *darkness*, no *harmony ... between Christ and Belial* (Satan), nothing *in common* between *believer* and *unbeliever*. The fifth question is the most critical and it indicates that there is no *agreement ... between the temple of God* (*i.e.* the locally gathered church) *and idols* (verses 15–16). These verses, let it be repeated, of themselves do not

---

[14] For discussion of the origin of the fragment and whether or not it was written by Paul, see Furnish, pp. 375–383, 140–147.
[15] Fee, *op.cit.*, p.157. [16] 1 Cor. 7:12–15. [17] 1 Cor. 10:27.
[18] 1 Cor. 14:22–25. [19] 1 Cor. 5:9–11.

call either for total separation from the world or for withdrawal from Christians with whom doctrinal differences exist. They all relate to the specific exhortation not to engage in idolatrous meals or services, which apparently (some of) the Corinthians had continued to do.

The key exhortation is now undergirded with Old Testament 'promises' (7:1). God lives in *the temple* or congregation[20] *of the living God* and *walks among* his *people* as their *God* (verse 16).[21] Therefore, Paul exhorts, *come out from them* (*i.e.* the idolators), *be separate*, and *touch no unclean thing* (*i.e.* the idols and temples; verse 17). Moreover, since God is a *Father* to his *sons and daughters* the same principle of withdrawal and separation applies (18). By 'promises' Paul means these Old Testament texts as quoted which teach that God lives among his people and that he is their Father.

Paul completes his mini-sermon with a final exhortation which takes its point of departure, as with the earlier component, from the initial call not to be mismated with unbelievers. Paul turns from exhorting the Corinthians and now also includes himself in the appeal *let us purify ourselves … perfecting holiness*. The church as the temple of God, in which he lives, is to be cleansed from any contact with the worship of other gods; the members are to perfect their *holiness out of reverence for God*. In the first letter Paul taught that, although there are no other gods, nevertheless to engage in the pagan meals is to share in worship of demons.[22] It is separation and purification from this that Paul is calling for here.

In conclusion, it should be emphasized that what is at stake here are fundamental truths about God, Christ and Christian commitment set in the context of a dark and seductive paganism. Paul's words continued to have application wherever Christians are potentially entangled in idolatry, the occult or pagan religious practices. Christians may be joined to unbelievers socially or by an existing marriage; they are not at liberty to participate in their religious worship.

3. Paul's appeal for reconciliation: conclusion (7:2–4)

Make room for us in your hearts. We have wronged no-one, we have corrupted no-one, we have exploited no-one. [3]*I do not say this to condemn you; I have said before that you have such a place in our hearts that we would live or die with you.* [4]*I have great confidence in you; I take great pride in you. I am greatly encouraged; in all our troubles my joy knows no bounds.*

[20] 1 Cor. 3:16.   [21] See Lv. 26:11–12; Hos. 1:10.   [22] 1 Cor. 10:20.

Paul now returns to his appeal for personal reconciliation with the Corinthians. Once again he urges them to *make room for us in your hearts* (verse 2), or more literally, to be 'expansive' in their attitude to him. The previous passage, relating to idolatry, possibly indicates that Paul was not favoured by either Jews or Gentiles among the Corinthians Christians. Many Gentiles, it seems, found his teaching on idolatry unnecessary and restrictive,[23] whereas the Jewish believers, especially as incited by the Judaizing newcomers, would perhaps feel that he had not gone far enough in his demands. In response Paul sets out the teaching on separation in a very clear manner and calls on the Corinthians to receive him in their hearts.

Without commenting on them in detail, Paul refutes three accusations currently being made against him, namely that he had *wronged* them, *corrupted* them and *exploited* them. We do not know exactly what the charges were, but they may have related to the collection of money for the believers in Jerusalem. Perhaps Paul is being charged with dishonesty and corruption in these matters. Nevertheless, he does not write this to *condemn* the Corinthians (verse 3). If they are saying these things it will be due to the evil slander of other people. Indeed, he sees his future and theirs as being closely connected in relation to death and life; Paul *would live or die with them* (verse 3). As believers together they share a common destiny.

Evidently, despite the problems, Paul remains both optimistic and confident of his relationships with them. He writes of his *great confidence* and *pride* in the Corinthians and says that, in spite of afflictions incurred through the ministry, he is greatly encouraged (verse 4). Here we have an insight into the remarkable resilience and perseverance of the apostle Paul, which doubtless he would quickly attribute, as we also should, to the grace of God and the power of the Spirit.

[23] *Cf.* 1 Cor. 10:23.

III   Paul in Macedonia: Titus' news from Corinth (7:5 – 9:15)

7:5–16
12.   Titus' news from Corinth: the 'sorrowful letter'

Prior to his 'long digression' about the ministry of the new covenant (2:14 – 7:4) Paul had appealed to the Corinthians to 'forgive and comfort' an offending member. Writing from Macedonia, Paul takes up the thread of his travel narrative which had been broken in Troas (2:12–13). He explains how relieved and thankful he had been to have finally heard of the Corinthians' support of him in their attitude to the offender.

For when we came into Macedonia, this body of ours had no rest, but we were harassed at every turn – conflicts on the outside, fears within. [6]But God, who comforts the downcast, comforted us by the coming of Titus, [7]and not only by his coming but also by the comfort you had given him. He told us about your longing for me, your deep sorrow, your ardent concern for me, so that my joy was greater than ever.

[8]Even if I caused you sorrow by my letter, I do not regret it. Though I did regret it – I see that my letter hurt you, but only for a little while – [9]yet now I am happy, not because you were made sorry, but because your sorrow led you to repentance. For you became sorrowful as God intended and so were not harmed in any way by us. [10]Godly sorrow brings repentance that leads to salvation and leaves no regret, but worldly sorrow brings death. [11]See what this godly sorrow has produced in you: what earnestness, what eagerness to clear yourselves, what indignation, what alarm, what longing, what concern, what readiness to see justice done. At every point you have proved yourselves to be innocent in this matter. [12]So even though I wrote to you, it was not on account of the one who did the wrong or of the injured party, but rather that before God you could see for yourselves how devoted to us you are. [13]By all this we are encouraged.

In addition to our own encouragement, we were especially delighted to see how happy Titus was, because his spirit has been refreshed by all of you. [14]I had boasted to him about you, and you have not embarrassed me. But just as everything we said to you was true, so our boasting about you to Titus has proved to be true as well. ¹⁵*And his affection for you is all the greater when he remembers that you were all obedient, receiving him with fear and trembling.* ¹⁶*I am glad I can have complete confidence in you.*

a. God comforts the downcast

Since sea travel had to be suspended for the winter months, we infer that Titus' non-arrival in Troas by late autumn left Paul with no alternative but to sail (on the last ship?) for Macedonia. Of the three known churches in Macedonia – Beroea, Thessalonica, Philippi – the latter is the most likely alternative rendezvous to have been previously agreed on by Paul and Titus. Paul may indeed have spent some time there awaiting the arrival of Titus and then writing this lengthy letter.

It would appear that Titus was the bearer of both good and bad news. On the one hand he told Paul that the disciplinary matter had been resolved satisfactorily, and that, while the Corinthians' support of the collection was disappointing, it could perhaps still be retrieved. On the other hand, however, Titus would have informed the apostle of the strengthening grip of the Judaizers on the Corinthian church and of the increasingly personal attacks which were being directed at Paul.

The time of waiting for Titus in Macedonia was one of suffering for Paul and his companions. His words *this body* (literally, 'flesh') *of ours had no rest* (verse 5) mean that sleep was denied them. Because of their ministry in the gospel, they were *harassed at every turn* (verse 5), that is, subjected to intense pressure. They experienced *conflicts on the outside* (Jewish or pagan persecution?) and *fears within* (worry about Titus' safety?). The deep distress which led Paul to leave Troas was in no way relieved by his arrival in northern Greece. Pain arising from his work as an apostle was to be his experience wherever he was – whether Corinth, Ephesus, Troas or Macedonia.

The despair of verse 5 is contrasted with the relief and thankfulness expressed in the next verses (6–7) commencing as they do with the words *But God*. Yes, Paul's pain and suffering had been great, 'but God...'. In referring to *God, who comforts*, Paul now echoes phrases he used at the beginning of the letter (1:3–7). Certainly his apostolic ministry had meant being *harassed* and *downcast*. Nevertheless, he could also testify to God having *comforted* him. While he is writing of the God of the Old Testament,[24] of his actions in the distant past, he is also testifying to the activity of that same God at that very time. God, this God, had comforted Paul in Macedonia! The God of the Bible, of yesterday, is the God of today, powerful and active to comfort his people.

God brought his comfort to Paul in a twofold manner. There was, first, the eventual arrival of Titus, thus removing fears that thieves had struck him down. (Possibly Paul had expected Titus to bring the collection with him, thus making him an attractive target for attack.) Further, to his immense relief, Titus brought an enthusiastic report of the positive Corinthian response to the 'sorrowful' letter. Titus was *comforted* by the Corinthians' *longing, sorrow* and *ardent concern* for Paul (verse 7). Thus Paul was *happy* at their reassurance to Titus of their loyalty towards Paul and of their deep regret at having caused him pain.

b. Their response: godly sorrow

Paul now reveals what he had previously hinted at. The reason for his upset state at Troas and Macedonia had been deep concern at the effects of the (now lost) letter to the Corinthians (2:1–4, 13). He now discloses *regret* (verse 8) at the severity of the letter. As their apostle, Paul felt a fatherly love towards his children in the gospel.[25]

Certainly the letter did *hurt* the Corinthians, though *only for a little while* (verse 8), and with a positive outcome: *godly sorrow* (verse 10). Paul here reminds his readers of two effects of sorrow or grief. There is *worldly sorrow* (verse 10), which is at best a shallow remorse, but which is consumed by bitterness and self-pity and which issues in *death*. Alternatively there is *godly sorrow* which produces *repentance* as expressed in *earnestness, eagerness, longing* and *concern* (verse 11) and which issues in *salvation* (verse 10).

There is a play on words here. The letter having been sent, Paul expresses *regret* at the painful effect he knew would follow. Now that the response has been so encouraging, as shown in their *godly sorrow*, he no longer regrets sending the letter. The Corinthians have expressed a *repentance* that leaves *no regret*.[26]

---

[24] Is. 40:1–2.
[25] 1 Cor. 4:14 – 15; 2 Cor. 6:13.
[26] Greek, *metamelomai* (verse 8) ... *ametamelēton* (verse 10).

c. The reason for sending the letter

Commentators are divided over the reason Paul originally wrote his lost letter. Some support the equating of this incident with the moral disciplinary problem set out in 1 Corinthians 5. Others believe there was a dispute between an individual (newly arrived?) in Corinth and Paul. The position is, however, that there is not enough data to be sure what the problem was. All we can deduce is that Paul speaks of it as *the matter* (verse 11) in which one person *did*, and another suffered, a *wrong* (verse 12, literally 'an injustice'). The opinion that Paul was the one who suffered the wrong seems unlikely in view of his reference to himself not as the other party, but as the third party (see verse 12).

As it turned out, the majority were well disposed towards Paul, as Paul had told Titus (verse 14), but they were, perhaps, slow to express their loyalty to him. But now the letter, which called for a demonstration of obedience in response to a particular problem person (or persons), had provoked an animated expression of *ardent concern* for Paul and his apostolic authority (verse 7: *longing, sorrow, ardent concern*: verse 11: *earnestness, eagerness, indignation, alarm, longing, concern, readiness to see justice done*).

It might be concluded that Paul was over-sensitive in this matter. However, it is clear (verse 12) that his primary intention was neither self-vindication nor the punishment of the offender. It was, rather, that the Corinthians' loyalty for Paul might come into sharp focus, not for his benefit, but for theirs.

Paul knew perfectly well what was at stake. To have rejected Paul would have implied the rejection of Christ whose 'authority' (*exousia*) Paul had been commissioned to exercise among them (10:8; 13:10). The threatening presence in Corinth of the Judaizers with their 'different gospel' (11:4) had the effect of placing the Corinthians' attitude to Paul on trial. Paul was thankful that their response to him had been overwhelmingly positive.

d. Titus in Corinth

Titus conveyed to his friend an exciting account of the Corinthians' welcome. They received him with *fear and trembling* while responding positively to his requests (verse 15), with the result that *his spirit* had *been refreshed* (verse 13) through his sojourn there. Such news *delighted* Paul (verse 13) and gave him a profound sense of relief. Paul was comforted in Titus' joy and peace at the Corinthian response. He *had boasted* to Titus of the Corinthians' loyalty (verse 14). So now his confidence is shown to have been well founded.

There is an astonishing contrast between Paul's earlier and present attitude. Earlier, in Ephesus he had been 'under great pressure, far beyond our ability to endure', having felt 'the sentence of death' (1:8–9). Then, even though delivered from this, when he came to Troas he 'still had no peace of mind', since there was no news about the Corinthians' reaction to the letter (2:13).

When he came to Macedonia he was *harassed at every turn – conflict on the outside and fears within* because Titus was not there. Clearly he had been deeply discouraged and depressed. But now, by contrast, he expresses in chapter 7 tremendous relief and rejoicing in what has happened among the Corinthians. The 'long digression' is so long that the remarkable change of mood is easily missed.

Unspoken but implied is Paul's renewed confidence in the power of God which had so clearly worked through the letter Paul had written. His new confidence arose out of the Corinthians' response to the 'sorrowful' letter. It is a serious mistake to underestimate the impact of the Word of God on those who hear and read it. To all appearances Paul was checkmated by the Corinthians' repudiation of his painful visit. His ministry there seemed to be at an end. And yet it was not finished. The living God is quite capable of changing apparently intractable attitudes (including ours!) by his Word and Spirit. Ministers of God's Word can find encouragement and renewal in their ministries by this example of the changed attitudes of the Corinthians.

e. God's comfort

God employs human agents to comfort his children. Paul expressed deep thanksgiving to God for his comfort through the brother Titus. It is good to recognize that God comforts us in this way and to thank him for the people he gives us as bearers of his comfort.

For our part we must ensure that we are loving, concerned and Christ-like people whom the 'God of all comfort' will employ in the comforting of those who are in distress. There is no lack of opportunity to comfort other believers within the body of Christ. One brother is unemployed, another is depressed about a difficult job situation; a sister has a chronically ill husband, another has rebellious children. The needs are there already within every congregation. Our eyes need to be open and our hearts generous with compassionate care. Above all we must resist the temptation to run away from people's needs because we do not think we can cope. The troubled do not usually expect us to solve their problems; but they do appreciate our concern and prayerful support. What matters most to people in distress is not 'saying things' but 'being there'.

8:1 – 9:15
13. Titus' news from Corinth: the collection

The transition from chapter 7 to chapter 8 is marked by a change of tone. In the former chapter Paul relives the joyous reunion in Macedonia with Titus who brought good news of the Corinthian response to the 'sorrowful letter' about the disciplining of the offender. Now, in chapter 8, he writes in more sober tones but yet with a real measure of encouragement and optimism about the other report brought by Titus from Corinth – news about the collection.

Chapters 8 – 9 relate to what Paul elsewhere calls 'the collection for God's people'[1] or, more elaborately, a 'contribution for the poor among the saints in Jerusalem'.[2] This 'contribution', finalized c. AD 57, had its beginnings a decade earlier in Jerusalem when Paul and Barnabas made a missionary compact with the Jerusalem church 'pillars', James, Peter and John. It was then agreed that James, Peter and John would evangelize Jews while Paul and Barnabas would go to the Gentiles. The one condition attaching to this missionary agreement was that Paul and Barnabas should 'remember the poor', that is, make provision from the Gentile churches for the poor among the Christians in Jerusalem.[3]

Paul explained to the Romans that the 'spiritual blessings' of the gospel enjoyed by the Gentile Christians have come to them from the Christian community in Jerusalem. The Gentiles owe them a spiritual debt which is to be repaid by 'material blessings'.[4] Implicit in the collection was Paul's desire to create a sense of unity and brotherhood between the two branches of Christianity, Jewish and Gentile, between whom there had been a measure of tension.

[1] 1 Cor. 16:1.   [2] Rom. 15:26.   [3] Gal. 2:9–10.
[4] Rom. 15:27.

Perhaps Paul, in particular, sought to demonstrate his bona fides in keeping his side of the agreement made at Jerusalem regarding 'the poor'. Hence it was appropriate that, near the end of his Aegean ministry, Paul should arrange for this collection.[5] In bringing this gift from the churches of Galatia, Asia, Macedonia and Achaia to the church in Jerusalem, Paul fulfilled the undertaking made to James, Peter and John ten (?) years earlier. It was a fitting end to this chapter in Paul's missionary career.

We may speculate that the impressive scale on which the collection was arranged may also have represented Paul's attempt to deal with problem of the Judaizers. The Judaizing party had been active at the time of the missionary meeting between Paul, Barnabas and the 'pillars' and also at the subsequent conference at Jerusalem between delegates from Antioch and the mother church.[6] At those two meetings, implicitly at the first and explicitly at the second, the Judaizing programme among the Gentiles was rejected. The Judaizing movement, however, did not disappear, and in recent days had manifested itself in the arrival in Corinth of the Jewish missionaries. This mission flourished in the climate created by James's leadership of the Jerusalem church, though it was not, apparently, authorized by him. Did Paul organize the collection on such a large scale to strengthen James's hand against a movement which originated in Jerusalem and which was now creating such havoc in the Gentile churches? Paul would thus have been able to say, 'We agreed to remember the poor; and now we have. You agreed that the Gentiles should not be troubled by the circumcision party, but they have been. We have kept our part of the agreement; you keep yours. Exhort or order the Judaizers to leave the Gentile churches alone.' While this is speculation, it is by no means unlikely or unreasonable.

Paul set out the arrangements for the collection in the first Corinthian letter: 'On the *first* day of every week, *each* one of you should set aside a sum of money in keeping with his income, saving it up, so that when I come no collections will have to be made. Then, when I arrive, I will give letters of introduction to the men you approve and send them with your gift to Jerusalem.'[7]

A year before the writing of 2 Corinthians, the Corinthian Christians had begun to put money aside, though it seems they had

[5] 1 Cor. 16:5–6; Acts 19:21; 24:17.
[6] Gal. 2:4–5; Acts 15:1, 5.   [7] 1 Cor. 16:1–4.

now become slack and irregular (8:10–11). So that the matter can be finalized by the time of his own coming to Corinth, Paul is dispatching Titus along with two unnamed colleagues, one of whom is well known, the other less well known (8:16–18).

Chapters 8 – 9, therefore, form a self-contained unit within the letter in which he seeks to encourage the readers to complete the collection arrangements. Was Paul successful? In his letter to the Romans, written some months later, he notes that 'Macedonia and Achaia were pleased to make a contribution for the poor among the saints in Jerusalem. They were pleased to do it...'.[8] We conclude, therefore, that the Corinthians did eventually fulfil their undertakings.

From these chapters we are able to discern some of the abiding principles which should control the Christian's stewardship of his gifts and resources. Further, we are warned in what Paul says not to be 'parochial', that is, preoccupied with the affairs of our own 'parish'. Believers are to look beyond the needs in their own particular congregation and to show concern for God's people in other places also.

1. The generous Macedonians (8:1–5)

And now, brothers, we want you to know about the grace that God has given the Macedonian churches. [2]Out of the most severe trial, their overflowing joy and their extreme poverty welled up in rich generosity. [3]For I testify that they gave as much as they were able, and even beyond their ability. Entirely on their own, [4]they urgently pleaded with us for the privilege of sharing in this service to the saints. [5]And they did not do as we expected, but they gave themselves first to the Lord and then to us in keeping with God's will.

Paul expressed deep appreciation for the Christians of Macedonia. The Thessalonians had undergone persecution, yet from them the gospel had echoed forth into the length and breadth of the Greek mainland, and beyond.[9] Paul will express his thanks to God for the Philippians' 'partnership in the gospel from the first day until now', by which he means that for more than ten years they had 'shared with me in the matter of giving and receiving'.[10]

In writing to one church, the Corinthians, Paul rather pointedly refers to the actions of other Christians, the Macedonians. They were so poor (verse 2) that Paul did not expect them to share in the

8 Rom. 15:26–27.   9 1 Thes. 1:6–8; 2:14; 2 Thes. 1:5.   10 Phil. 1:5; 4:15.

collection arrangements. In response to the gospel *they gave themselves first to the Lord and then to us* (verse 5). It is not Paul but they who have raised the matter. They have begged for *the privilege* (*charis*, grace) of *sharing in this service* (or ministry) *to the saints* (verse 4). Some of Paul's most penetrating insights are expressed in passing, as here when he describes the heart of Christian commitment as *they gave themselves first to the Lord and then to us*. In response to the gospel we are, indeed, to 'give' ourselves to the Lord Jesus and to his ministers and other believers. Committed self-giving to the Lord and to others is basic to Christianity.

Paul's main message to the Corinthians is painfully clear. The Corinthians, who were (relatively speaking) rich, had agreed to contribute, but they had now ceased. The Macedonians, who were extremely poor, actually asked to contribute, and had begun to do so. Paul is attempting to shame the Corinthians into proper action.

The word *charis* is used twice in this passage: *grace* (verse 1) and *privilege* (verse 4). Just as God shows grace or unearned love towards sinful and unworthy people, so the Macedonians show grace or unconditioned kindness to the faraway Christians in Judaea. The latter is an illustration of the former, showing that, in one of its meanings, grace displays God's attitude of uninvited favour towards sinners (see 6:1). But *charis* also means God's unearned mercy dynamically working within us. Hence, Paul writes of *the grace that God has given the Macedonian churches* (verse 1). Let the Corinthians imitate the Macedonians in showing grace towards others, and it will be able to be said of them that the grace of God is also at work within them.

The *charis*, the *grace* of God towards them and also dynamically at work in them, will create *charismata*, gifts, within them, including the gift of giving.[11] The rediscovery in recent years of the gifts of God within the churches is most welcome. Where members of a congregation are expressing the grace of God displayed towards them by a gracious exercising of gifts for others, there we see a church which can truly be called 'charismatic'.

Certainly it will come as a great surprise to many to discover that generous giving to support others is a 'gift'. Have we heard of believers praying to receive this gift? (!) Yet a 'gift' it most assuredly is, and, like other gifts as listed in the New Testament,[12] one that is to be used in love for the good of others.

[11] Rom. 12:8.
[12] See Rom. 12:3–8; 1 Cor. 12:6–11, 27–31; 13:1–3; Eph. 4:11–13; 1 Pet. 4:7–11.

2. The mean Corinthians (8:6–11)

So we urged Titus, since he had earlier made a beginning, to bring also to completion this act of grace on your part. [7]*But just as you excel in everything – in faith, in speech, in knowledge, in complete earnestness and in your love for us – see that you also excel in this grace of giving.*

[8]*I am not commanding you, but I want to test the sincerity of your love by comparing it with the earnestness of others.* [9]*For you know the grace of our Lord Jesus Christ, that though he was rich, yet for your sakes he became poor, so that you through his poverty might become rich.*

[10]*And here is my advice about what is best for you in this matter: Last year you were the first not only to give but also to have the desire to do so.* [11]*Now finish the work, so that your eager willingness to do it may be matched by your completion of it, according to your means.*

Paul exhorts the Corinthians in tones of warm encouragement. Since they *excel* at so many things – *in faith, in speech, in knowledge, in complete earnestness* – let them also *excel* in their generosity (verse 7). But there is no element of coercion or command. They have the example of the Macedonians. Let the Corinthians now give expression to their love.

Paul places before the Corinthians another example of *grace*. The first example, the Macedonians, had been poor; the second, the Lord Jesus Christ, had been, like the Corinthians, rich. *You know the grace (charis) of our Lord Jesus Christ*, wrote Paul (verse 9), indicating that this was something they *already* knew. The teaching was not new, though the application may have been.

This text, surely one of Paul's most powerful, teaches that Jesus' personal existence did not begin with his birth in Bethlehem in the last years of Herod the Great. The words *he was rich* indicate an unlimited pre-existence,[13] while the words *he became poor* speak of his entry into the stream of history at a particular time and place.[14] Paul's letter to the Philippians contains a good explanation of the phrase *he was rich*. There he states that Jesus was (in his pre-existence) 'in very nature God,' and that he possessed 'equality with God'.[15] In other words, Jesus was, in his essential being, all that God was. In this way Jesus 'was rich', eternally so. The words *he became poor*, which relate to his human life, serve to point up the greatness of the wealth of that former existence in contrast to his incarnate life.

[13] 'He was' is actually a present participle in the Greek: 'being rich'.
[14] The aorist tense of the verb 'to be poor' indicates a specific, completed action.
[15] Phil. 2:6.

143

Philippians 2 also helps to explain Paul's words *he became poor* and *his poverty*. In that passage Jesus 'made himself nothing, taking the very nature of a servant' and 'humbled himself and became obedient to death – even death on a cross'.[16] Jesus' *poverty*, therefore, was his humility in incarnation and life, and his obedience in death. Jesus himself said, 'Foxes have holes and birds of the air have nests, but the Son of Man has nowhere to lay his head.'[17] He knew from the beginning that in Jerusalem there awaited him the 'cup' of suffering and the 'baptism' of death.[18] Paul's words *he became poor* describe Jesus' humble life and obedient death which, as Brunner observed, were an 'indissoluble unity'.[19]

Nevertheless, as Denney noted, 'The New Testament knows nothing of an incarnation which can be defined apart from its relation to atonement.' He continued, 'Not Bethlehem but Calvary is the focus of revelation.'[20] Packer comments: 'The crucial significance of the cradle at Bethlehem lies in its place in the sequence of steps down that led the Son of God to the Cross of Calvary.'[21]

Another text which helpfully illuminates the words *he became poor* and *his poverty* is found earlier in this letter, where Paul writes of the death of Christ: 'God made him... to be sin' (5:21). It is through the poverty of that sacrificial, reconciling death that we sinful paupers become, in him, *rich* in the righteousness of God.

We may discern a twofold application of our great Christmas text, 2 Corinthians 8:9. First, we need gladly to receive the Lord Jesus Christ in our hearts, thankful for his sacrificial saving work on our behalf. Secondly, in all matters related to giving and gifts we ought to imitate his generosity. Clearly the self-giving death of Jesus is a major motive for our generosity.

3. Generosity, love and the cross

Congregations, like people, have personal characteristics. A little reading between the lines indicates that Macedonian congregations were quite different from the Corinthian congregation. The churches in Macedonia had displayed great generosity despite their deep poverty. By contrast, although they were probably prosperous, the

---

[16] Phil. 2:6–8.   [17] Lk. 9:58.
[18] Mk. 10:39.   [19] E. Brunner, *The Mediator* (Lutterworth, 1963), p. 399.
[20] J. Denney, *The Death of Christ* (Tyndale Press, 1960), p. 179.
[21] J. I. Packer, *Knowing God* (Hodder and Stoughton, 1973), p. 51.

Corinthians had proved to be tight-fisted.

A study of the letters to the Macedonians[22] and the Corinthian churches reveal further striking characteristics. The Corinthians were quick to form factions, take one another to court, and to parade their spiritual gifts.[23] They were slow to show consideration to their poor and weak members.[24] They tolerated, even boasted in, flagrant immorality on the part of some of their members.[25] When new ministers from Judaea arrived, they quickly lost interest in Paul in favour of these more interesting new arrivals (11:4). Their selfishness and fickleness are written on every page of Paul's letters to them. The Macedonians, however, though not without their difficulties, reveal themselves to be more concerned and caring congregations. The Philippians sent Paul money for his ministry and, on one occasion, the gift of a personal companion.[26] Paul is only once able to commend the Corinthians for showing love, and even then he is being somewhat charitable towards them (8:7). So lacking were they in love that it was necessary for Paul repeatedly to exhort the Corinthians to show love.[27] By contrast, Paul commends the Macedonian churches for their loving behaviour.[28] The Macedonians were full of love, and, in spite of their poverty, very generous. The Corinthians lacked both love and generosity. Perhaps it is significant that despite their esteem for 'wisdom'[29] it was necessary for Paul to explain to the Corinthian churches at such great length the meaning of the grace of God and the death of Christ. Apparently they did not understand what it meant either to be loved or to show love.

4. Equality (8:12–15)

For if the willingness is there, the gift is acceptable according to what one has, not according to what he does not have.

[13]*Our desire is not that others might be relieved while you are hard pressed, but that there might be equality.* [14]*At the present time your plenty will supply what they need, so that in turn their plenty will supply what you need. Then there will be equality,* [15]*as it is written: 'He who gathered much did not have too much, and he who gathered little did not have too little.'*

---

[22] The Thessalonians and Philippians.
[23] 1 Cor. 1:12; 6:1; 13:1–3.   [24] 1 Cor. 11:21.   [25] 1 Cor. 5:2.
[26] Phil. 4:16; 2:25–30.   [27] 1 Cor. 13:1–3; 14:1; 16:14; 2 Cor. 8:8, 24.
[28] 1 Thes. 1:3; 3:6; 2 Thes. 1:3; Phil. 1:9; 2:1.
[29] 1 Cor. 1:20.

What is important in the exercise of gifts, in this case the giving of money, is *willingness* to share what one has with other people. The poor widow, whom the Lord commended for giving the two copper coins,[30] was poor in resources; but she was rich in *willingness* to share from what she possessed. It is this attitude which the apostle is commending here (verse 12).

a. Equality of readiness

It is not that he was expecting the Corinthians to be sole donors (verse 13). It is, Paul affirms, to be a matter of *equality* (verse 14). He does not mean exact *material* equality as in an enforced *per capita* method of contributing which would reduce everyone to the same economic basis; it is a *spiritual* equality which is in mind. Clearly, if it is 'by force' it cannot be 'by grace'. According to the varying resources of each, there should be an equal *willingness* to give so that one brother does not coast along at the expense of the too-great sacrifice of another. It is to be an *equality* of *willingness*.

Paul illustrates his principle of *equality* or spiritual fairness by the quotation from Exodus 16:18 which refers to the Lord's provision of manna in the wilderness. By God's miraculous working, those who had little and those who had plenty *both* had sufficient. Paul's point is that wherever God's people, however well or poorly endowed, are prepared to use their gifts and money willingly, there will be *equality*; there will be no injustice. Some may have more and others less, but all will have enough.

The application arising from this is clear. We should, according to our resources, fulfil the principle of 'fairness' or *equality* by *willingness* to share. Specifically, we must search our conscience to ensure that some fellow Christian is not having to do more or pay more in the fellowship of believers because we, selfishly, are doing less or paying less that we could. It may be that our missionaries who represent us or our pastors who serve us are suffering overwork or under-remuneration (or both) on account of our failure to share with *equality* and *willingness*.

b. Paul as a spiritual leader

Clearly Paul was facing the kind of ticklish problem which many a

[30] Mk. 12:42–44.

Christian leader has subsequently faced. The Corinthians were falling behind in their giving. That the failure lay in the area of money is a detail which is not finally important. It could equally have been that they were deficient in the area of prayer or evangelism. The question was, how are those who have the task of spiritual leadership to encourage a greater response from fellow believers? Paul's approach to the dilatory Corinthians, therefore, is instructive.

First, he gives them credit for having *begun*; though he diplomatically but clearly reminds them that there had been a shortfall. Titus, who possibly possessed financial acumen,[31] would bring this matter to finality (verse 6).

Secondly, he notices approvingly their *other* gifts in which they excel, though he firmly but gently indicates that their generosity fell behind the exercise of gifts which more readily attracted attention (verse 7).

Thirdly, he resists the temptation to manipulate their guilt or to impose a legalistic requirement upon them. God's grace to them must remain the motive; their graciousness is to be the response (verse 8). Since Paul makes no mention of the Old Testament practice of tithing, we may conclude that Paul did not regard this as a practice binding on Christians.

Fourthly, he holds up for their self-examination and self-comparison, two living models of graciousness. The former, the Macedonians, were much poorer in every way than the Corinthians (verse 2). The second model, the Lord Jesus, was immeasurably rich in his pre-incarnate Sonship with the Father (verse 9). The Corinthians were not as rich as the Lord or yet as poor as the Macedonians. Yet they, the Corinthians, were lacking in generosity when any kind of real cost was involved. The implications were obvious.

Fifthly, he adopts the stance of an advisor. He gently conveys to them that the shortfall is their problem, not his. He can only advise; they, and only they, can resolve the problem (verse 10). It is fundamental to the task of 'helping' (or counselling) that the person helped should face up to his problem and not be allowed to manoeuvre the helper into the position where *he* has to resolve the problem.

TITUS' NEWS FROM CORINTH: THE COLLECTION

5. Honourable arrangements (8:16–24)

I thank God, who put into the heart of Titus the same concern I have for you. [17]*For Titus not only welcomed our appeal, but he is coming to you with much enthusiasm and on his own inititative.* [18]*And we are sending along with him the brother who is praised by all the churches for his service to the gospel.* [19]*What is more, he was chosen by the churches to accompany us as we carry the offering, which we administer in order to honour the Lord himself and to show our eagerness to help.* [20]*We want to avoid any criticism of the way we administer this liberal gift.* [21]*For we are taking pains to do what is right, not only in the eyes of the Lord but also in the eyes of men.*

[22]*In addition, we are sending with them our brother who has often proved to us in many ways that he is zealous, and now even more so because of his great confidence in you.* [23]*As for Titus, he is my partner and fellow-worker among you; as for our brothers, they are representatives of the churches and an honour to Christ.* [24]*Therefore show these men the proof of your love and the reason for our pride in you, so that the churches can see it.*

No-one knew better than Paul that his initiative in instituting the collection would lay him open to the accusation that the money was destined for his pocket. Indeed, to this day few things are so destructive of the credibility of the ministry as the implication of covetousness and dishonesty.

What Paul was administering was a *liberal gift* (verse 20), that is, a sizeable amount. To preserve his credibility he took every precaution to dissociate himself from any direct contact with the money. 'When I arrive', he told the Corinthians, 'I will give letters of introduction to the men you approve and send them with your gift to Jerusalem.'[32] When the collection was finally delivered to Jerusalem, seven envoys from various churches accompanied the money.[33] The concept of the collection was bigger than the person of Paul. In the meantime, to expedite its conclusion in Corinth he is sending not one, or even two, but three persons to supervise.

Titus needs little introduction. He is Paul's *partner* and *fellow-worker*, and yet he is also a minister in his own right, since he is going to the Corinthians *on his own initiative* (verse 17).

The second person is called *the brother who is praised by all the churches for his service to the gospel* (verse 18). The Macedonian churches have *chosen* him (verse 19; the verb suggests 'by a show of hands').

Possibly Titus will read the letter to the church and introduce this person to the Corinthians. Who is he? One possibility is that this

[31] See Gal. 2:1 (*cf.* Acts 11:29–30), where Titus, with Paul and Barnabas, brought financial assistance from Antioch to Jerusalem.
[32] 1 Cor. 16:3.   [33] Acts 20:4.

famous evangelist among the Macedonian churches was Luke. That Luke, the author of Acts, was present in Philippi (from which this letter was possibly written) from AD 50 to 57 may be inferred from the first 'we/us' passage in Acts which ends at Philippi and the second such passage which begins at Philippi.[34] It is quite possible that Luke remained at Philippi throughout those eight years and had become famous in the region. One who was capable of writing the gospel, as Luke was, may well have been famous for his preaching of the gospel.

The third person is referred to as *our brother who has often proved to us in many ways that he is zealous* (verse 22). Titus will also, presumably, introduce him to the Corinthians.

These latter two persons are designated *brothers* (verse 23),[35] which is a semi-technical title for those who work closely with Paul under his leadership. Paul refers to them as *representatives* (literally 'apostles') *of the churches* (verse 23), by which he means agents or couriers appointed by him, who 'shuttle' between himself and the churches.

In the NIV, verse 23 concludes by saying that these representatives are *an honour to Christ*. More accurate, however, is the RSV translation, 'messengers of the churches, the glory of Christ' (*doxa Christou*). The churches, not the brothers, are the 'glory of Christ'. This is perhaps similar in thought to John's vision of Christ as holding in his right hand the 'seven stars',[36] which probably means the seven churches. If this is a correct interpretation, we are to understand the local church as a (potential) source of brightness or glory for Christ. The challenge will be for our local church to bring glory to Christ by its lifestyle and witness.

These verses, then, are in effect a mini-letter of commendation of these three Christians to the Corinthians church. They serve to remind all Christians and church leaders to exert extreme care in all matters relating to church money.

6. To save face (9:1–5)

There is no need for me to write to you about this service to the saints. ²For I know your eagerness to help, and I have been boasting about it to the Macedonians, telling them that since last year you in Achaia were ready to give; and your enthusiasm has

[34] Acts 16:11–17; *cf.* 20:6.
[35] See E.E. Ellis, 'Paul and his Co-workers', *NTS* 17 (1971), pp.437–453.
[36] *E.g.* Rev. 1:16.

stirred most of them to action. ³But I am sending the brothers in order that our boasting about you in this matter should not prove hollow, but that you may be ready, as I said you would be. ⁴For if any Macedonians come with me and find you unprepared, we – not to say anything about you – would be ashamed of having been so confident. ⁵So I thought it necessary to urge the brothers to visit you in advance and finish the arrangements for the generous gift you had promised. Then it will be ready as a generous gift, not as one grudgingly given.

The initial 'willingness' or *eagerness* of the Corinthians to contribute was the factor which inspired the Macedonians to offer to share the collection (verse 2). Now, however, Paul is evidently embarrassed. What the Corinthians were initially enthusiastic to do they have not yet completed, though their goodwill in the matter is undiminished. Lest Paul be *ashamed* – to say nothing of the Corinthians (verses 3–4) – he exhorts that the arrival of the three representatives bearing this letter be the occasion for bringing the collection swiftly to its completion. However, while Paul is clearly laying some moral pressure on the Corinthians, under no circumstances does he want the collection to be *grudgingly given*; as such it would not arise out of grace. It is to be a *generous gift* (verse 5).

It may be that Paul deliberately chose to write a letter, rather than come in person. A written message would give the Corinthians more time to respond graciously, whereas his physical presence with them would be threatening. If this were the case, and it is a matter of surmise, the written word provided for the possibility of a willing response, whereas the word spoken by one present with them might have provoked a forced response.

7. Areas of giving

Paul's teaching about the 'contribution for the saints' raises the question about other areas of Christian giving mentioned by the apostle. There are at least three such areas.

a. The support of the Christian teacher

From Galatians we learn that those who receive instruction (literally, 'are catechized') in the Word are to share (literally, 'fellowship') their good things with their instructors. In writing to the Corinthians, Paul said that those who sow 'spiritual seed' have the right to reap 'a material harvest'. It was the command of the

Lord that 'those who preach the gospel should receive their living from the gospel'. The apostle instructed Timothy that the teaching elder was a 'labourer' who 'deserved his wages'.[37]

From these passages it is clear that the minister is under obligation to teach (and to do so thoroughly), and the congregation is to support him financially (and to do so adequately). The practice of canvassing non-church people to support Christian ministry appears to be excluded by Paul's teaching. It is the one who is taught who is obliged to 'fellowship' with the teacher. Where the people have the quality of 'willingness' referred to previously, there will be no inequality.

b. The support of the missionary

Paul thanked God for the Philippians' 'partnership in the gospel from the first day until now.'[38] The time span represented by that verse is more than ten years. At the very beginning the Philippians sent him money at Thessalonica, then subsequently at Corinth. Now more recently, imprisoned in Rome a decade or so later, they dispatched money and a companion.[39]

Sadly, many congregations lose touch with their missionaries with the passing of the years and the change of minister. Perhaps a small but active committee could be created in many churches to ensure a two-way flow of communication and care between missionary and congregation. Meanwhile, the Philippians' partnership 'from the first day until now' remains a helpful example for us.

c. The care of those in need

Paul taught the Ephesian readers that the thief must steal no more, but do useful work instead, so that he may have something to share with those in need.[40] Through our labours many of us have more than we need. But to what extent do we give to those in need? Instead, those who have one house buy a holiday home; those who have progressed from black and white to colour television add a video; those who have an ordinary oven want a microwave too. The surplus is for sharing; but few of us do so.

The poor among the Jerusalem saints were in need through the

[37] Gal. 6:6; 1 Cor. 9:11–14; 1 Tim. 5:17–18.
[38] Phil. 1:5.   [39] Phil. 4:14–18; 2 Cor. 11:9.   [40] Eph. 4:28.

151

effects of a famine in Palestine which began *c.* AD 46. We can imagine how widespread the effects were. The raising of 'the collection', therefore, coincided with a time of serious need. Grievous illness and hunger in our fellow human beings must always be met by kindness and generosity, as Jesus taught in his parable of the good Samaritan.[41]

The section following, verses 6–15, applies immediately to the 'contribution'. However, they apply equally to the areas of giving we have discussed.

8. Sowing and reaping (9:6–15)

Remember this: Whoever sows sparingly will also reap sparingly, and whoever sows generously will also reap generously. [7]*Each man should give what he has decided in his heart to give, not reluctantly or under compulsion, for God loves a cheerful giver.* [8]*And God is able to make all grace abound to you, so that in all things at all times, having all that you need, you will abound in every good work.* [9]*As it is written:*

> *'He has scattered abroad his gifts to the poor;*
> *his righteousness endures for ever.'*

[10]*Now he who supplies seed to the sower and bread for food will also supply and increase your store of seed and will enlarge the harvest of your righteousness.* [11]*You will be made rich in every way so that you can be generous on every occasion, and through us your generosity will result in thanksgiving to God.*

[12]*This service that you perform is not only supplying the needs of God's people but is also overflowing in many expressions of thanks to God.* [13]*Because of the service by which you have proved yourselves, men will praise God for the obedience that accompanies your confession of the gospel of Christ, and for your generosity in sharing with them and with everyone else.* [14]*And in their prayers for you their hearts will go out to you, because of the surpassing grace God has given you.* [15]*Thanks be to God for his indescribable gift!*

a. The manner of giving; generously and cheerfully

God's grace towards us reproduces his graciousness within us. Since God's grace towards us is infinite and not measured out, we who receive it are to show generosity without measurement or calculation. We are not under compulsion. Thus ours is to be a ready, not a reluctant, response. *God loves a cheerful giver* (verse 7) because he is himself a cheerful giver (*cf.* verse 15). Nevertheless, Paul is not

---

[41] Lk. 10:25–37.

encouraging his readers to be either casual or impulsive givers. Each person *should give what he has decided in his heart to give* (verse 7). Inward resolve is to be followed by decisive and cheerful giving.

The use of church envelope schemes has much to commend it. It requires the giver to think about the amount he is to give and it helps him to be regular in his giving, even when he is unavoidably absent from church. It also preserves confidentiality, something the Lord enjoined.[42]

What are my motives for donating money for Christian purposes? Am I seeking to relieve my guilt? Is it a 'pay-off' to avoid some avenues of Christian service which I am unwilling to fulfil? Is it to be thought super-spiritual by those who notice how much I contribute? Various faulty motives may inspire us to give generously, but only a real appreciation of God's grace to us can prompt us to give 'cheerfully'.

b. Giving is sowing

Paul certainly knew the tight-fisted Corinthians. Clearly they were in his mind as he wrote *Whoever sows sparingly will also reap sparingly* (verse 6). By this farmers' proverb Paul introduces a thought-model which he will develop in verses 6–10. Implicit in the proverb is the bountiful generosity of God seen in sowing and harvesting. Provided the weather and such factors are favourable the farmer could expect from each wheat seed sown a harvest of thirty, sixty or even one hundred seeds.[43] Therefore *whoever sows generously will also reap generously* (verse 6).

From such a harvest, Paul teaches, *in all things at all times* they will have *all that* they *need* and also *will abound in every good work* (verse 8). Just as the God of harvest gives the sower enough harvest to supply seed next season, his daily bread, and some surplus beyond that, so God the fruitful provider will bless the generous giver with enough for his needs and will also *enlarge the harvest of* his *righteousness* or 'multiply (his) resources' (RSV) for good works (verse 10). God provides the giver with enough for his needs and with more than enough to continue sharing with others.

Such a person is the embodiment of the godly person portrayed in Psalm 112:9 who 'scatters abroad his gifts to the poor' (*cf.* verse 9). This person is blessed with numerous and upright descendants, with

---

[42] Mt. 6:2–4.   [43] Mk. 4:20.

prosperity, with clear guidance in life and with courage. The apostle has the whole Psalm in mind, not merely the verse he quotes. If the Corinthians then, or we today, had modelled our lives on Psalm 112, this entire section of the letter would be unnecessary.

c. The results of giving

Three results of generous giving may be discerned in verses 10–15. The generous giver will be further blessed with a *harvest of ... righteousness* (verse 10). God will continue to bless this person with both the means and opportunity for graciousness. He will be *enriched ... for great generosity* (verse 11). As Harris puts it, 'The greater the giving, the greater the enrichment. The greater the enrichment the greater resources to give.'

In recent times there has arisen a 'theology of prosperity' which teaches that God will bless with health and riches those who give generously in support of Christian ministry. In the Old Testament it is clear that the multiplication of resources was viewed as the blessing of God. In the last chapter of Job, God gave the faithful sufferer twice the prosperity he enjoyed before the onset of his troubles.[44] In the New Testament, however, this enrichment is reinterpreted as spiritual fruitfulness[45] and caring support in the family of Christians.[46] The prayer in 3 John 2 that the readers may enjoy good health and success has many parallels in non-Christian literature and should be seen merely as a pious wish couched in conventional terms. What Paul promises to the generous giver is not wealth-in-return but *all that you need* and also sufficient for *every good work* (verse 8).

Secondly, their giving mediated through Paul *will result in thanksgiving to God* (verse 11). As the hungry saints receive food they will raise their hearts and voices in *many expressions of thanks to God* (verse 12). Through the givers and through the organizer Paul many will *praise God* (verse 13). When we opt out of giving, we opt out of the privilege of meeting human needs and also deny ourselves the honour of promoting God's glory.

Significantly, Paul never deviates from the truth that God saves us by his free grace and not through good works such as giving. Thus giving is a *proof* (verse 13) or an 'acknowledgment' of the

[44] Jb. 42:10–17.   [45] Eph. 1:7–8; Col. 2:2.
[46] Gal. 6:10.

gospel of Christ. Such goodness is the confirmation of our salvation, but not its basis.

Thirdly, such practical kindness will establish a bond of affection and prayer between giver and receiver. Though separated by distance and culture, they now enjoy a fellowship whose visible expression is the money given and received (verse 14). The receivers perceive that in the graciousness of the giver may be discerned the outworking of the grace of God in them (verse 14). Both giver and receiver will know that God's grace, embodied in Christ, has started a chain reaction of generosity, thanksgiving and fellowship. Hence Paul *thanks … God for his indescribable gift* (verse 15), Jesus Christ his Son, which has begun it all.

While the apostle is referring to generosity in gifts of money, we may validly apply his principles to the exercise of all God's gifts. Having prayerfully consulted our friends to help us ascertain our gifts from God, we will then readily, generously and cheerfully seek to exercise such gifts as a grateful expression of his saving grace towards us. It will be our certain experience that the faithful Lord of the harvest will enrich us beyond our expectations.

IV   Paul's third visit to Corinth (10:1 – 13:14)

10:1 – 11:15
14.   Defence against criticism

In this part of 2 Corinthians Paul turns to answer the biting criticisms of the new ministers and their supporters within the Corinthian church. It is clear from what is written that Paul, his ministry and his doctrines were under wholesale attack. For his part he viewed with the utmost seriousness the presence of these 'apostles' among the Corinthians. It is not too much to say that Paul's very apostolic relationships with the Corinthians was now at stake, to say nothing of their future as a Christian congregation.

1.   Their criticism: Paul's weapons are worldly (10:1–7a)

By the meekness and gentleness of Christ, I appeal to you – I, Paul, who am 'timid' when face to face with you, but 'bold' when away! [2]I beg you that when I come I may not have to be as bold as I expect to be towards some people who think that we live by the standards of this world. [3]For though we live in the world, we do not wage war as the world does. [4]The weapons we fight with are not the weapons of the world. On the contrary, they have divine power to demolish strongholds. [5]We demolish arguments and every pretension that sets itself up against the knowledge of God, and we take captive every thought to make it obedient to Christ. [6]And we will be ready to punish every act of disobedience, once your obedience is complete. [7]You are looking only on the surface of things.

The Corinthians, or a group of them, have been captivated by these outwardly impressive ministers from Judaea. Power and prestige lay at the heart of their ministry. They brought letters of recommendation (3:1) and pointed to ecstatic and visionary experiences to legitimize their claims (5:13; 2:1). They boasted of the distance they had travelled in coming to Corinth (10:13–18).

The newcomers and their Corinthian friends despised Paul, as is evident from his self-defence offered throughout these latter chapters. In chapter 10 the dominant objection is that he is authoritative only when away, through his letters. When present he is *'timid'* (verse 1), not a quality they valued. To them Paul was a worldly minister (verses 2 and 3), lacking *divine power* in anything he did (verse 4).

It is probable that their perception of Paul arose directly from his quite deliberate presentation of himself. That he was *'timid'* was due entirely to his imitation of *the meekness and gentleness of Christ* (verse 1), qualities which Jesus specifically pointed to in the famous invitation to the 'weary and burdened'.[1] That he was 'worldly' probably means that Paul did not pretend to be more than an ordinary man. There was nothing to Paul beyond what could be seen and heard (*cf.* 12:6). His 'power' was to be experienced only in the gospel he spoke, not in himself. Of himself he was nothing, nobody; quite mundane, really. The new ministers, however, apparently presented themselves as powerful and extraordinary. Throughout history many ministers have sought to make an impact on people in terms of their supposed powers and paranormal qualities. Christians and congregations, by failing to see that God's power is found in his Word, are vulnerable to ministers who possess or claim to possess extraordinary power. In despising his humility and his ordinary humanity, his critics revealed that it was in fact they, not Paul, who were worldly in their perceptions and therefore lacking in the true power of God.

Moreover, the Corinthians (or some of them) were gravely mistaken in their underestimation of the strength of human rebellion against God, something Paul likens to the owner of a powerfully guarded fortress, apparently impenetrable to outside attack. Paul's weapons, despised as they were in Corinth, so far from being 'worldly' actually possess *divine power to demolish strongholds* (verse 4) and *arguments and every pretension that sets itself up against the knowledge of God* (verse 5). Paul's ministry, unassuming as it was in personal terms, was capable of taking *captive every thought to make it obedient to Christ* (verse 5).

We do well to follow Paul in his realistic estimate of the entrenched power of unbelief and pride in the human mind. Only the right weapons will subdue and capture this proud fortified rebel

[1] Mt. 11:29

who places himself over God; those right weapons are the words of the gospel.

Like Paul, we are so to proclaim Jesus Christ as Son of God, as crucified to save sinners, as Lord and as judge, that *every thought* of the hearer is captured to obey *Christ*. Let it be said that preaching, whether based on the New Testament or the Old Testament, whether exegetical or thematic, fails at its most critical point if it does not on every occasion bring the claims of the Lordship of Christ and his saving power into the clearest focus. Only this gospel can *make* that which *sets itself up against the knowledge of God*, namely rebellious unbelief, *obedient to Christ*. Paul's very humility, which they despise, what he calls *the meekness and gentleness of Christ* (verse 1) indicates that he is himself a man whose *every thought* is *captive* to obey *Christ*. He is the living embodiment of what he proclaims.

2. Paul's apostolic authority (10:7b–11)

If anyone is confident that he belongs to Christ, he should consider again that we belong to Christ just as much as he. [8]For even if I boast somewhat freely about the authority the Lord gave us for building you up rather than pulling you down, I will not be ashamed of it. [9]I do not want to seem to be trying to frighten you with my letters. [10]For some say, 'His letters are weighty and forceful, but in person he is unimpressive and his speaking amounts to nothing.' [11]Such people should realise that what we are in our letters when we are absent, we will be in our actions when we are present

To Paul's critics in Corinth, matters of personal ministry style were uppermost. What kind of person was he when absent, as a letter-writer? What was he like when present with them in person? In their eyes he was a disappointment wherever he was. His letters they found 'frightening' (verse 9); they thought he set out to intimidate them. This contrasted strongly with his 'timidity' when face to face (verse 1) which was, to them, a complete let-down. He was like some canine guardians, 'all bark and no bite'!

Paul's test of ministry here, and elsewhere, is congregational, not charismatic. He invited the Corinthians, as they actually hear his letter being read, to 'Look at the obvious facts' (verse 7a, margin), that is, at the reality of the Christian congregation at Corinth (3:1–3; 5:11–13). The existence of a community of Christian believers, founded by Paul, is powerful evidence that the 'weapons' he fought with 'have divine power' (*cf.* verse 4).

One unnamed person in particular is *confident* (overconfident?) *that he belongs to Christ* (verse 7), that is, that he is a Christian minister. Presumably this person, who was probably not a newly arrived minister but a Corinthian, was a leading critic of Paul. Let him *consider again* (verse 7) that Paul also is a minister; the very church congregation in which he sits is proof of that!

A straightforward one-to-one comparison between Paul and this unnamed rival is not possible. Paul cannot get away from the special commission given to him by the exalted one on the road to Damascus.[2] There *the Lord gave* to Paul his *authority for building up* (verse 8) churches like that at Corinth. Against those who wish to apply personal or stylistic tests to him Paul points back to his unique and historic commission by the risen Lord and to the tangible evidence of that in the continuing existence of congregations of Gentile believers. Paul's unusual words *If I boast somewhat freely ... I will not be ashamed of it* (verse 8) probably echo the vocabulary of his critics as they seek to promote their ministry against his. Paul is simply stating that the Damascus Road commission is the basis for all that he does in ministry and he is not ashamed of it.

The unnamed rival, in particular, has enunciated a powerful criticism of Paul which is now quoted in the letter. The words *some say* could be taken as 'he says', and have been so understood, as coming from this critic of Paul.[3] This critic says Paul's *letters are weighty and forceful but in person he is unimpressive and his speaking amounts to nothing* (verse 10). To that point Paul had written three letters to the Corinthians; the present letter was the fourth. The complaint is that the letters are what he should be in himself, weighty and forceful. But he is not that; far from it. When he does finally come it is an anticlimax. Physically he is *unimpressive and his speaking* is beneath contempt.

When analysed, this criticism relates to Paul's physical appearance and his *speaking* or voice. Unfortunately our only information about Paul's stature is far removed from our period and of uncertain reliability.[4] Paul may have been unimposing and unimpressive. He may have lacked the high professionalism of the much-vaunted orators of the day. Possibly he suffered from some disability or

[2] Gal. 1:11–16; Acts 22:21; 26:17–18.

[3] See Barrett.

[4] According to the *Acts of Paul and Thecla* (second century) Paul was 'a man of small stature with bald head and crooked legs'.

160

deformity. (Is the 'thorn in the flesh' in mind here? 12:7–8.[5]) Whatever is being referred to, Paul's critics seized hold of it together with his stubborn preference for supporting himself rather than receiving their patronage (11:7–11) as fatal objections to his genuineness as an apostle. The Greek world admired physical beauty and leisure, while despising imperfection and manual labour. In terms of Greek values, Paul the tentmaker, of amateurish speech and doubtful appearance, had little to commend him. Before he became a noted orator the young Demosthenes was subjected to ridicule in Athens on account of his poor physique and weak voice. This had to be rectified by a long and rigorous programme of physical and vocal exercises.[6] 'He corrected his lisp and his indistinct articulation by holding pebbles in his mouth while he recited long speeches and he strengthened his voice by running or walking uphill … reciting speeches … in a single breath.'[7] This indicates the seriousness with which physical bearing and public speaking was viewed in the Greek world. To Greek eyes Paul was very inferior.

However, rejoins Paul, let this man reflect on the true situation. In reality Paul's ministry is exactly the same wherever he is – whether *absent*, by letter, or *present*, in person (verse 11). What he says *in his letters* he *will be in* his *actions* when he is with them.

3. Missionary comparisons (10:12–18)

We do not dare to classify or compare ourselves with some who commend themselves. When they measure themselves by themselves and compare themselves with themselves, they are not wise. [13]*We, however, will not boast beyond proper limits, but will confine our boasting to the field God has assigned to us, a field that reaches even to you.* [14]*We are not going too far in our boasting, as would be the case if we had not come to you, for we did get as far as you with the gospel of Christ.* [15]*Neither do we go beyond our limits by boasting of work done by others. Our hope is that, as your faith continues to grow, our area of activity among you will greatly expand,* [16]*so that we can preach the gospel in the regions beyond you. For we do not want to boast about work already done in another man's territory.* [17]*But, 'Let him who boasts boast in the Lord.' For it is not the one who commends himself who is approved, but the one whom the Lord commends.*

Paul turns now from his Corinthian critic to the visiting 'apostles'

---

[5] *Cf.* Gal. 4:13–14 where the Galatians were not contemptuous of Paul's unnamed bodily ailment.

[6] See Plutarch, *The Age of Alexander* (Penguin, 1973), pp. 189–193.

[7] *Ibid.*, p.197.

who, it seems, are making comparisons within their group and between their group and Paul. The new 'ministers' are making much of the various distances they have travelled to come to Corinth, and in particular of the fact that they have come a greater distance than Paul. They have travelled (apparently) from Palestine; Paul has been in the Aegean area for about seven years now.

Paul's response is twofold. First, he refers to the missionary concordat made a decade earlier in Jerusalem in which it was agreed that James, Peter and John should go to the Jews while Paul and Barnabas would take the gospel to the Gentiles.[8] This agreement established *the field God has assigned* (verse 13) to the two missionary enterprises. The Greek word *kanōn*, translated *limits* (verses 13, 15) and *field* (verse 16) originally applied to a carefully specified area in which local communities were obliged to provide donkeys and carts as public transport for Roman officials who were passing through.[9] Paul has *come as far as* the Gentile Corinthians *with the gospel of Christ* (verse 14), as agreed at the meeting. He *confines* his *boasting to the field God has assigned* (verse 13). As Jews (11:22) these persons are *going too far in their boasting* (verse 14) and have encroached beyond their *territory*, and are *boasting about work already done* (verse 16), that is by Paul, among Gentiles. This conflict has some of the marks of a modern industrial demarcation dispute. Bluntly, these people who are boasting of the distance they have travelled have encroached into his agreed field of labour.

Secondly, Paul regards the whole exercise of comparison as futile. Comparison as a rhetorical device was widely practised among the Greeks.[10] We also see an example among Jews in the Pharisee's favourable comparison of himself to the publican, in the parable told by Jesus.[11] Since the newcomers were 'Hebrews' (11:22), it is likely that their comparisons arose from Jewish rather than Greek practice. Paul's references to it (verse 12), however, were in Greek categories in accordance with the understanding of his readers.

In Paul's view it is pointless to authenticate or disqualify ministries on the basis of comparison of self-commendation. *It is not the one who commends himself who is approved,* he observes, *but the one whom the Lord commends* (verse 18).

[8] Gal. 2:7–9.

[9] See G. H. R. Horsley, *New Documents Illustrating Early Christianity* (Macquarie University Press, 1981), pp. 36–45.

[10] C. B. Forbes, 'Comparison, Self-Praise and Irony', *NTS* 22 (1986), pp. 1–30.

[11] Lk. 18:9–14.

Letters of recommendation and appeal to ecstatic gifts or mission-ary travels[12] are examples of self-commendation. The existence of the Corinthian church, established by Paul, is Paul's letter of recommendation, sent by Christ (3:1–3). Let the Corinthians look at themselves (*cf.* verse 7) and they will see the Lord's commendation of Paul's ministry. In passing, it is significant that Paul makes so little of 'signs and wonders', which he unquestionably performed, as legitimizing his ministry. For Paul, the demonstration of the genuineness of his ministry was that he 'persuaded people' (to become Christians) and that congregations of believers, 'living letters', had come into existence (5:11–13). Those modern ministers who seek proof of their true ministry in the miraculous and the extraordinary are really following Paul's opponents, not Paul.

4. Paul's reply: 'I promised you to Christ' (11:1–4)

I hope you will put up with a little of my foolishness; but you are already doing that. I am jealous for you with a godly jealousy. ²I promised you to one husband, to Christ, so that I might present you as a pure virgin to him. ³But I am afraid that just as Eve was deceived by the serpent's cunning, your minds may somehow be led astray from your sincere and pure devotion to Christ. ⁴For if someone comes to you and preaches a Jesus other than the Jesus we preached, or if you receive a different spirit from the one you received, or a different gospel from the one you accepted, you put up with it easily enough.

By the authority of Christ who made him an apostle, Paul has *promised* the Corinthians to their Lord (verse 2). Earlier he depicted himself as the slave of a conquering general (2:14), as the 'aroma of Christ' (2:13), as the 'postman' of Christ (3:3), as an 'ambassador' of Christ (5:20), and as a fortress-conqueror (10:4–5). Now he depicts himself as a 'matchmaker' who has introduced the Corinthians to Christ as his fiancée. As the good friend of the groom-to-be, he is keeping watch over the bride-to-be until the groom comes to consummate the marriage (verse 2).

This is a profound allegory of the church, the Lord and the Christian evangelist. The bride-to-be is the church; the husband, soon to come, is the heavenly Lord; the matchmaker who is concerned for the bride's fidelity is the evangelist. Paul is alarmed that the bride-to-be is flirting with *a Jesus other than the Jesus we preached* (verse 4), and is dangerously close to being unfaithful to the

[12] 2 Cor. 3:1–3; 5:11–13; 10:12–18.

true Jesus. As the *serpent* lured *Eve* away from God,[13] so, by inference, these teachers of a false gospel are enticing the bride-to-be away from a *sincere and pure devotion to Christ* (verse 3). *The serpent's cunning* (verse 3) was his plausible speech. The *cunning* of these teachers was their alternative but false gospel and their charismatic power.[14] It is clear from this passage that the pure gospel alone joins us to, and keeps us in a right relationship with, Christ. A sincere devotion to Christ is possible only where the true and authentic gospel of Christ is taught and heard (verse 3). Christians need to think about *what* they are being taught rather than being impressed by *who* is teaching them, however winsome he or she may be.

Paul has made some reference to the jibes of his critics that he is 'worldly' and 'timid' (10:1–4). Now he takes up another, that he is a *fool* (verses 1, 16, 21, literally, a mind-less person). Evidently his critics have mockingly commended the Corinthians for 'putting up with that fool Paul' (*cf.* verse 1). Paul is deeply hurt by this, hence the ironical quote, 'You gladly put up with fools' (verse 19). At one level Paul is referring to himself, while at a deeper level, if they only knew it, to the visiting missionaries. For, using the same verb, he remarked of the Corinthians' reception of the new people that they *put up with* them *easily enough* (verse 4). 'You tolerantly *put up with* me as a fool,' Paul is saying, 'even though it was I who betrothed you to Christ. Meanwhile you gladly *put up with* these people even though they, in the service of their own interests, lead you away from Christ' (*cf.* 11:20–21).

In these verses Paul gives three reasons why the Corinthians should 'put up with him', each introduced in the Greek by 'for', which the NIV translates only once.[15] First, as apostle and evangelist he feels divine jealousy for the Corinthians at this time of spiritual danger for them (verses 2–3). Secondly, the Corinthians are vulnerable to falling away from Christ through their interest in an untrue gospel (verse 4). Thirdly, Paul states that he is in no way inferior to these 'super-apostles' (verse 5).

It was, therefore, very important that the Corinthians should 'bear with' Paul. Barrett writes that Paul 'recognises a real danger that his work in Corinth may be lost, and that the church there may perish'. That they were tolerating these 'apostles', while rejecting Paul, was in fact placing them in the greatest spiritual jeopardy.

---

[13] Gn. 3:1–6.   [14] *Cf.* Rom. 16:17–18.   [15] See Harris.

5. The hyper-men (11:5–6)

But I do not think I am in the least inferior to those 'super-apostles'. [6]I may not be a trained speaker, but I do have knowledge. We have made this perfectly clear to you in every way.

Who were these 'super-apostles' who 'preach a Jesus other than the Jesus we preached'?

Paul cannot be referring to *the* apostles, since he himself had already stated that he and they preach the same gospel focused on the death, burial, resurrection and appearances of Christ.[16] Rather, he is referring to those recently arrived 'apostles' who claim superiority over Paul on the basis of the greater distances they have travelled (10:12–13) and on the 'abundance of revelations' they have experienced (12:1, 7). He concedes no superiority to these ministers.

Paul has chosen (or invented) his word 'superlative' *(hyperlian)* with care.[17] Within chapters 10 – 13, where he particularly inter-acts with his opponents, there are a number of compound words formed of *hyper*, 'above', 'beyond'. Paul writes of their missionary imperialism 'going too far', as '*over*extending' themselves (10:14; *hyperekteinein* into 'regions *beyond*' (10:16; *ta hyperekeina*). They boast of 'surpassingly great revelations' (12:7; *tē hyperbolē tōn apocalypseōn*) and the resultant 'super-elation' or 'conceit' *(hyperairesthai)*. To expose their boastfulness Paul boasts of being 'more' a servant of Christ (11:23: *hyper*), by which he means one who has suffered greater ignominy. Truly Paul's opponents are hyper-men, aptly described as 'very superior', *hyperlian*. It was their belief, apparently, that God's power would come upon their power, making them men of hyper-power. In their eyes Paul had no power of his own and therefore none from God; he was quite power-less, 'weak' and lacking in 'competence' (*cf.* 3:5-6; 11:21).

Such is the modern preoccupation with power and miracles in some circles that the minister who lacks these things is regarded as inferior or not genuine. In an earlier passage, however, Paul made it clear that the weapons he fought with, namely the gospel, were not at all worldly but had divine power to capture the rebellious mind to

[16] 1 Cor. 15:11; *cf.* 3–5.

[17] The word 'super-' or 'superlative' (rsv; Greek, *hyperlian*) occurs in the New Testament only here and at 12:11. In fact the word cannot be found elsewhere until medieval times. It is conceivable that Paul coined the word, which is made up of *hyper*, 'above', and *lian*, 'very much'. The word is ironic and means something like 'very superior'.

make it obedient to Christ (10:3–6). It is the gospel, not the miraculous, which is the power of God.[18]

His admission that he is *not ... a trained speaker* probably relates back to the unnamed Corinthian critic of the previous chapter and his jibe about Paul's 'weak' physical presence and 'contemptible' speech. It should not be inferred that the 'super-apostles' were. eloquent orators.

At that time educated people in major Hellenistic cities such as Corinth were greatly taken by those who were impressive public speakers. We note the great interest shown by the Corinthians in Apollos' oratory. Orators trained their voices for hours on end like opera singers and learned literally hundreds of rhetorical speaking devices, a few of which (such as comparison, simile and metaphor) are still recognized today. While Paul's letters reflect considerable rhetorical skill, he was, for some reason, unimpressive as a speaker, what he calls (literally) a 'layman in speech'.

Paul has just denied any inferiority to the 'super-apostles'; why does he now concede deficiency in public speech? It is, I believe, so that he can claim the more strongly to be in no way deficient or inferior in *knowledge*. This is not, of course, a claim to superior education or to intellectual distinction as such, but to the true knowledge of the true gospel given to Paul on the Damascus Road and confirmed subsequently by the Jerusalem apostles.[19] It was by means of knowledge, false knowledge, that the Corinthians were in such grave danger. How important that they (and we) recognize the distinctive and authoritative knowledge of Paul in matters relating to Jesus and the gospel.

6.   Paul and the Corinthians' money (11:7–11)

Was it a sin for me to lower myself in order to elevate you by preaching the gospel of God to you free of charge? [8]*I robbed other churches by receiving support from them so as to serve you.* [9]*And when I was with you and needed something, I was not a burden to anyone, for the brothers who came from Macedonia supplied what I needed. I have kept myself from being a burden to you in any way, and will continue to do so.* [10]*As surely as the truth of Christ is in me, nobody in the regions of Achaia will stop this boasting of mine.* [11]*Why? Because I do not love you? God knows I do!*

It is evident from these words that the Corinthians were at that time deeply offended that he had not accepted payment from them for his

[18] Rom. 1:16.   [19] *Cf.* Gal. 1:18–19; 2: 7–9; 1 Cor. 15:11.

166

earlier ministry among them. Possibly this old wound[20] had been opened by the presence of the new ministers in Corinth, who were evidently receiving money for their ministry (cf. 11:20; 2:17). His question *Was it a sin?* (verse 7) indicates the depth of bitterness about this matter.

When he had worked among them six years earlier he had been prepared to accept support from the Macedonians (verse 9) but not from the Corinthians. In their minds this could only mean that he loved the Macedonians but did not *love* the Corinthians (verse 11), that he preferred people from the province of Macedonia to the province of Achaia. (Was there, perhaps, an underlying inter-provincial rivalry which Paul's actions magnified, at least in their minds?) His answer *God knows I do! (love you* – verse 11) was obviously heartfelt, in view of the great pain they had caused him over the years. The problem was, in reality, that they were not opening their hearts to him (6:11–13), preferring even false apostles to him (11:1, 4, 19–20).

A possible further factor was that Paul had so blatantly disregarded social convention. At that time it was customary for the wealthy to put other people under obligation by gifts and favours. The practice of patronage was deeply embedded in Graeco-Roman society. The expectation was that the affluent gave money to travelling philosophers and that this was received without question and with due deference and gratitude to one's patron. In declining the Corinthians' gifts Paul was, from their viewpoint, in serious breach of social convention.[21]

Paul's 'sin' was that while he had specifically sought to include the wealthy in his ministry,[22] he had not only declined their money, but worse, he had actually done manual work to support himself. By 'lowering himself' (verse 7) in physical labour, which the Greeks traditionally despised, Paul evangelized them, thus 'elevating' them or lifting them out of the morass of their former evil lifestyle.[23] The newcomers claimed to be dispensers of a 'superior' ministry, but in reality it had been through the 'weak and foolish' ministry of Paul that the Corinthians had been uplifted.[24]

[20] It is clear from 1 Cor. 9:6, 14 that this had been an issue earlier.
[21] For an example of the deference clients showed patrons, see G. H. R. Horsley, *op.cit.*, pp. 56–57.
[22] Acts 17:4, 12; Rom. 16:1, 23; 1 Cor. 1:26; 11:22.
[23] *Cf.* 1 Cor. 6:9–11.
[24] The word 'elevate' continues Paul's word-play on the root *hyper – hypsōthēte.*

167

Paul does not give his reasons for declining to accept financial support in Corinth. One likely consideration in his mind may have been that Corinth, due to its position and wealth, was plagued with visiting money-hungry prophets and philosophers. In provincial, unsophisticated Macedonia the apostle could perhaps accept support without compromising the gospel, but not in *the regions of Achaia* (verse 10).

7. The new missionaries and their mission (11:12–15)

And I will keep on doing what I am doing in order to cut the ground from under those who want an opportunity to be considered equal with us in the things they boast about.

[13]*For such men are false apostles, deceitful workmen, masquerading as apostles of Christ.* [14]*And no wonder, for Satan himself masquerades as an angel of light.* [15]*It is not surprising, then, if his servants masquerade as servants of righteousness. Their end will be what their actions deserve.*

So far from altering his decision to receive money for ministry in Corinth, the activities of the new ministers have in fact reinforced Paul's policy. *I will keep on doing what I am doing,* he says, *in order to cut the ground from under* his opponents (verse 12). Having come all the way to Corinth, as Paul had, these people proposed that they were, at the very least, all that Paul was. Thus they declared themselves to be *apostles of Christ* (verse 13), *servants of righteousness* (verse 15) and servants of Christ (verse 23). The vocabulary of 'ministry' and 'apostleship' which Paul applied to himself they also applied to themselves, probably in deliberate imitation.

Possibly the word *righteousness* is critical here, indicating perhaps a key element in the Judaizing mission to reinstate the law and repair the damage believed to have been done to it by Paul.[25] So far from opposing the law of God, however, Paul upheld it.[26] To him, the law was upheld through the coming of the new covenant in which God imputed 'righteousness' to man. Righteousness was not achieved through keeping the law, but through the vicarious death of God's Son (3:9; 5:21). Paul, the apostle of Christ, is engaged in the 'ministry that brings righteousness' (3:9).

What Paul so strongly objects to and what underlies his strong language is that these *workmen*[27] were *deceitful* (verse 13). Their

---

[25] See Acts 21:21; Rom. 3:8; *cf.* 3:1–2; 6:1–2; 11:1. [26] Rom. 3:31.
[27] *Cf.* Mt. 9:37–38; 1 Tim. 5:18.

'deceit' is that they were *masquerading as apostles of Christ* and *servants of righteousness* (verses 13, 15). This reference to *'masquerade'* may refer to the ecstatic speech (5:13), the visions and revelations (12:1, 7) and the miracles (12:12) with which they clothed themselves in coming to Corinth.

In reality, however, they are *servants* of *Satan* (verses 14–15). The statement that *Satan himself masquerades as an angel of light* (verse 14) may refer to certain Jewish legends which told of Satan coming to and deceiving Eve in the disguise of an angel.[28] Their interest in *righteousness*, that is, to law-keeping, gave the appearance of morality and *light* (verse 14); but it is only an appearance, a disguise. The truth is that so far from being *apostles of Christ*, honest *workmen, servants of Christ*, they are *false apostles, deceitful workmen, servants* of *Satan*.

8. Paul's language

In these days, when toleration is regarded as a virtue, Paul's descriptions of the newcomers (*e.g.* 11:13) appear harsh. And yet his words express 'godly jealousy' (11:2)[29] for God's people. Clearly the Corinthians were in grave danger, through their welcome of these men, of severing their relationship with Christ. Despite their claims to be Christian ministers (11:23), the newcomers, as agents of Satan, were capable of causing at Corinth a falling away from God similar to that which the serpent caused in the garden of Eden (11:3). Clearly they attacked Paul's gospel as containing extraneous elements; presumably they also questioned the Corinthians' experience of the Spirit (*cf.* 4:2–3).

The grim history of religious wars and sectarian disputes has, thankfully, led to a deep desire for peace among Christian people. But is there not a danger of so over-reacting that we are prepared to sacrifice God's truth for any notion of unity? Christians can have no part in either bigotry or bitterness. But at the same time, it is right for them to hold tenaciously to the truth of God as revealed in Scripture and to resist all Satan's efforts to reclaim his former captives through false teaching.

Paul's harsh words about these false teachers are in keeping with the attitude of Scripture elsewhere toward the false prophet and the false teacher.[30] It is a serious matter to receive false teaching, but it

[28] See further Furnish.   [29] See Hos. 2:19–20; 4:12; 6:4; 11:8.   [30] Jas. 3; 2 Pet. 2.

169

is more serious by far to teach as true about God what is, in fact, false.

We may note in passing that in this letter Paul reveals a threefold pattern of activity by Satan. First, Satan seeks to divide and weaken the body of Christ, by bitterness and unforgiveness (2:10–11). Secondly, Satan seeks to maintain sinners in their spiritual blindness, unable to see the glory of Christ (4:4). Thirdly, Satan, above all, seeks to sever the believer from Christ by means of false doctrine about Christ (11:3, 14).

Regarding Satan, Christians are first to understand his strategy (which is clear from the activities mentioned above) and secondly to resist him with all the spiritual resources at their disposal, whereupon he will be put to flight.[31]

[31] Jas. 4:7; cf. 1 Pet. 5:8–9.

11:16 – 13:14
15. The weak fool

Accusations have been made that Paul is worldly, a fool, and weak. Paul denies the first: the weapons of his warfare are not worldly but possess divine power to capture the proud for a life of obedience to Christ (10:4). He then turns to their second and third accusations, that he is a 'fool' and 'weak'. With these he actually agrees, though his agreement, which combines both charges into one, is stated in a brilliant literary form, full of pathos.

1. Christ's fool (11:16–33)

I repeat: Let no-one take me for a fool. But if you do, then receive me as you would a fool, so that I may do a little boasting. [17]*In this self-confident boasting I am not talking as the Lord would, but as a fool.* [18]*Since many are boasting in the way the world does, I too will boast.* [19]*You gladly put up with fools since you are so wise!* [20]*In fact, you even put up with anyone who enslaves you or exploits you or takes advantage of you or pushes himself forward or slaps you in the face.* [21]*To my shame I admit that we were too weak for that!*

What anyone else dares to boast about — I am speaking as a fool — I also dare to boast about. [22]*Are they Hebrews? So am I. Are they Israelites? So am I. Are they Abraham's descendants? So am I.* [23]*Are they servants of Christ? (I am out of my mind to talk like this.) I am more. I have worked much harder, been in prison more frequently, been flogged more severely, and been exposed to death again and again.* [24]*Five times I received from the Jews the forty lashes minus one.* [25]*Three times I was beaten with rods, once I was stoned, three times I was shipwrecked, I spent a night and a day in the open sea,* [26]*I have been constantly on the move. I have been in danger from rivers, in danger from bandits, in danger from my own countrymen, in danger from Gentiles; in danger in the city, in danger in the country, in danger at sea; and in danger from false brothers.* [27]*I have laboured and toiled and have often gone without sleep; I have known hunger and thirst and have often gone without*

171

food; I have been cold and naked. [28]*Besides everything else, I face daily the pressure of my concern for all the churches.* [29]*Who is weak, and I do not feel weak? Who is led into sin, and I do not inwardly burn?*

[30]*If I must boast, I will boast of the things that show my weakness.* [31]*The God and Father of the Lord Jesus, who is to be praised for ever, knows that I am not lying.* [32]*In Damascus the governor under King Aretas had the city of the Damascenes guarded in order to arrest me.* [33]*But I was lowered in a basket from a window in the wall and slipped through his hands.*

a. Boasting

Through Christian influence on Western values, boasting is regarded as brash and impolite. Humility and self-effacement have traditionally been regarded as virtues. In Paul's day it was quite otherwise. People in Graeco-Roman antiquity possessed no hope of glory in an after-life. A detached immortality was the most one could expect. Therefore it was customary to achieve 'glory' in this life, and to boast of one's achievements in this life. Thus citizens and soldiers, without embarrassment and as a social convention, outdid one another in boasting of military and political achievements. These were listed on monuments or public buildings, depicted in household murals, or set forth in epic narratives. A good example is the *Res Gestae* of the Emperor Augustus in which he proudly recounts his many victories, official positions in Roman society, successfully completed buildings and other accomplishments Boasting was also commonplace among the Jews. The Pharisee in the temple boasted of his religious achievements.[1] Echoes of earlier boasting are evident in ex-Pharisee Saul's *curriculem vitae* in his letter to the Philippians.[2]

It seems likely that Paul's opponents made their claims over the Corinthians and their superiority over Paul in terms of the conventional lists of achievements about which they could boast Hence Paul writes, *since many are boasting in the way world does, I too will boast* (verse 18). They have left him no alternative; but Paul's boasting will be quite different.

b. Paul's Jewishness

At one point only does Paul seek to match his critics – their

---

[1] Lk. 18:9–12.   [2] Phil. 3:4–6.

Jewishness (verse 22). Are they *Hebrews?*[3] So is he. Are they *Israelites* by race?[4] So is he. Do they trace their lineage back to *Abraham?* So does he. In these matters he is equal with the newcomers. Why is Paul at such pains to establish this? Presumably it is because the Saviour and salvation originated among the Jews.[5] Not to have been a Jewish apostle would in the nature of things have been a fatal defect in one who claimed to represent the Messiah Jesus.

c. Foolishness and weakness

In everything else, however, Paul highlights matters of difficulty and hardship – hard work, imprisonment, floggings, threats to his life. What manner of boasting is this? In what must have been a daring exercise in antiquity, Paul takes the literary convention of boasting and inverts it. His boast is in folly, weakness, disappointment and defeat. One of the Roman soldier's most glorious achievements in battle, the *corona muralis*, was awarded for being the first over the wall of the city under siege. As Christ's fool, Paul boasts of being lowered *down* a wall as a fugitive (verses 32–33).

Paul's opponents boast of superiority (11:5; 12:11), of being 'super-apostles'. Yet the effect of their ministry is to enslave and manipulate those who succumb to them (verse 20). Paul, however, is the servant of Christ in his ministry to the churches. As opposed to the triumphalism of these newcomers, the essential character of Christ is the meekness and gentleness of a crucified slave. Christ's glory is his divinely humble service of others. This is the message of the cross which Paul seeks to embody and express in his ministry of evangelism.

Paul's list of 'accomplishments' (verses 22–33) is the longest of three such lists in 2 Corinthians,[6] though only here does he boast, in detail, of what had happened to him. He begins by stating that he *worked much harder*, had *been in prison more frequently* and *flogged more severely* than his opponents (verse 23). Those 'super-apostles', who surpass him in all things, say he is a *fool*. He agrees with them but claims to be more than a fool, in fact to be *out of* his *mind* (verse 23). Let them see how mad he really is. He has been *exposed to death again and again* (verse 23), giving examples of flogging, rod-beating,

---

[3] A word used for those who were descended from the patriarchs.
[4] That is, those who were by race and religion Jewish.
[5] Jn. 4:22.   [6] See 4:8–9; 6:4–10.

173

stoning, shipwreck, and being adrift at sea (verses 24–25). In his
many journeys there have been numerous dangers in crossing rivers,
evading robbers, escaping from enemies – Jew and Gentile alike
(verse 26). He has *laboured and toiled and ... often gone without sleep*; he
has *known hunger and thirst and ... often gone without food;* he has *been
cold and naked* (verses 27–28). And day by day there has been the
anxiety for the churches – not least the Corinthian church![7]

Only some of these incidents are found in the Acts of the
Apostles. We ought not to think therefore that when we have read
what Luke says about Paul we know everything about the apostle.
This list shows us how much more happened to him. The two
previous lists tell us how 'the ministry' (4:1; 6:3) brought suffering
to Paul. In this list of sufferings Paul speaks as *'a servant of Christ'*
(verse 23). The different English words 'ministry' and 'servant'
conceal their similarity in the original. Paul is a minister (*diakonos*)
who is engaged in ministry (*diakonia*). Paul is a minister of Christ
(verse 23) who is engaged in the ministry of reconciliation (5:18)
which brings peace between God and sinners through the death of
Christ. It is the faithful pursuit of this ministry which brought Paul
into the suffering of which he has spoken. He admits to being the
'fool' his opponents say he is. Paul is Christ's fool and proud of it.

In referring to his *concern for all the churches* (verse 28) he
particularly has in mind the *weak* Christian, that is, the one who is
likely to *be led into sin* (verse 29).[8] We can be certain that the
presence of false teachers in the Corinthian church had caused Paul
considerable anxiety for the well-being of vulnerable new Christians.
Here is an insight into the deep pastoral concern of Paul for the
churches. As one who confessed to being *weak* he stands with the
weak or 'vulnerable' new believers. He *inwardly burns* at the prospect
of such Christians falling away from Christ. We are reminded how
Christ who called himself 'gentle and humble'[9] identified with and
ministered to the little ones and the children.[10]

The newly arrived 'apostles' claim to have travelled greater
distances in coming to Corinth (10:12–14). Can they match this list
of sufferings incurred in the course of his ministry and from which
God did not shield him?'

---

[7] C. H. Spurgeon once commented that 'we have ... evils as numerous as these which Paul
included in his famous catalogue of trials: and ... one peril which he does not mention,
namely the perils of church meetings, which are probably worse than perils of robbers'.
[8] See 1 Cor. 8:11–13.   [9] Mt. 11:29.   [10] Mt. 18:1–6, 10–14.

d. Paul's example of leadership

This passage teaches us two things about Paul as an example. The first is that as Christians we are humbly to serve others in the gospel. Paul possessed the Christ-given authority to be an apostle. He exercised this ministry faithfully and yet he remained a humble servant and truly human. The great apostle is a good example of one to whom authority was given but who did not become manipulative or authoritarian.

The application to Christian ministers is clear. It is a temptation to use one's position (for instance, 'rector' or 'pastor') or one's gifts (such as leadership ability), or both, to create a circle of admirers. Such a person exercises his ministry in the name of Christ but is really involved in an 'ego trip'. More subtly, the minister may encourage people to lean on him like a crutch, out of his own need to be needed. Alternatively, the minister is capable of being corrupted by the power given him in the church so that he becomes a bossy authoritarian who must always have his own way. It must always be remembered that the word 'minister' means 'servant'.

The application is able to be extended to all people whose roles in life give them power over others – parents, employers, business executives, doctors, teachers, lecturers, and many more. The Christian must not shrink from exercising whatever authority his role gives him. But he must do so in a way that creates an environment of justice and fair play. And he himself must at all times remain, like Christ and the apostle, a humble servant. Further, this passage teaches us about the zeal of Paul which disregarded both discomfort and pain. Paul's zeal raises the questions about *our* zeal; *my* zeal in particular. Are we not embarrassed by the lack of it in the church and in ourselves? Let us be reminded about the source of Paul's zeal. It was on the one hand his clear grasp of the meaning of the death of Jesus, who had 'died for all' (5:14) as evidence of Jesus' love for all. It was this sense of being loved by Christ in his death that took Paul across flooded rivers and into many near-death experiences. On the other hand Paul, knowing the 'judgment seat of Christ', before which all must stand, vigorously 'persuaded' people to embrace Christianity (5:10–11). Let the love and fear of Christ which 'controlled' Paul also control us and kindle the fire of zeal within us.

175

2. Paul's 'thorn' (12:1–10)

I must go on boasting. Although there is nothing to be gained, I will go on to visions and revelations from the Lord. [2] I know a man in Christ who fourteen years ago was caught up to the third heaven. Whether it was in the body or out of the body I do not know – God knows. [3] And I know that this man – whether in the body or apart from the body I do not know, but God knows – [4] was caught up to paradise. He heard inexpressible things, things that man is not permitted to tell. [5] I will boast about a man like that, but I will not boast about myself, except about my weaknesses. [6] Even if I should choose to boast, I would not be a fool, because I would be speaking the truth. But I refrain, so no-one will think more of me than is warranted by what I do or say.

[7] To keep me from becoming conceited because of these surpassingly great revelations, there was given me a thorn in my flesh, a messenger of Satan, to torment me. [8] Three times I pleaded with the Lord to take it away from me. [9] But he said to me, 'My grace is sufficient for you, for my power is made perfect in weakness.' Therefore I will boast all the more gladly about my weaknesses, so that Christ's power may rest on me. [10] That is why, for Christ's sake, I delight in weaknesses, in insults, in hardships, in persecutions, in difficulties. For when I am weak, then I am strong.

a. Revelations

Paul turns now to a question which had apparently been flung at him: 'What *visions and revelations* could Paul claim as credentials for his ministry?' (see 12:1). Paul's reply is curious. It is as if he is unwilling to identify himself as the man who had the revelations. Thus he writes *I know a man* (verse 2), referring to himself not personally but impersonally; not in the first but in the third person. Though he *was caught up to the third heaven* (verse 2) – or *paradise* (verse 4),[11] he gives no detail (as his opponents have?) about the place of the *body* in this experience (verse 4). (Did ancient ecstatics believe they were lifted out of the body during these revelations?) It was, to be sure, a remarkable experience and yet it happened as long ago as *fourteen years* (verse 2). Paul had many visions,[12] but the one referred to here was apparently very spectacular. It may be possible to boast on behalf of *this man* (verses 3, 5) who experienced this revelation *fourteen years ago*, but of the Paul who was now writing to them he would boast only in *weaknesses* (verse 5), in the

[11] 2 Enoch 8:1. Paradise was the home of the righteous dead.

[12] Acts 9:12; 16:9–10; 18:9–10; 22:17–21; 23:11; 27:23–24. See further R. P. Spittler, 'The Limits of Ecstasy, in *Current Issues in Biblical and Patristic Interpretation*, ed. E. Hawthorne (Eerdmans, 1975), pp. 259–266.

disappointments and hardships listed in the previous chapter.

Paul is saying: 'I want you to look at what I am, not what I was. The man I want you to take into account is not the one who experienced an astonishing revelation then but the one you see now, in all his weakness', *so no-one will think more of me than is warranted by what I do or say* (verse 6). In this passage Paul is responding to the new missionaries who are pointing, apparently, to ecstatic experiences as a demonstration of their claims over the Corinthians as against the place of Paul. By his reply Paul rejects accreditation by ecstasy. The simple fact is that Christ commissioned Paul to be their apostle, and the demonstration of that did not lie in the display of ecstatic power, but in the reality of weakness as lived out before the Corinthians.

b. The 'thorn'

To the catalogue of weaknesses previously given, Paul now adds his most painful experience. It is not about the 'revelation' which *caught him up* (verse 2) that he will boast, but about the pain which brought him lowest of all, the *thorn* (verse 7). What was this *thorn*? The Greek word is *skolops*, which can mean either a 'stake' which pegged him to the ground or a 'splinter' (or thorn) which constantly irritated him. The word was employed in both senses. H. Minn comments that it conveys 'the notion of something sharp and painful which sticks deeply in the flesh and in the will of God defies extraction. The effect of its presence was to cripple Paul's enjoyment of life, and to frustrate his full efficiency by draining his energies.'[13]

Scholars have made many suggestions about the nature of Paul's 'thorn'. Was it persecution, sensual temptation, a speech defect, an ophthalmic disorder, epilepsy or one of the many further possibilities? It may be wise to take the view of Hughes, who observes: 'The very anonymity of this particular affliction has been ... productive of far wider blessing ... than it would have been the case had it been possible to identify ... the specific nature of the disability.'

Revelation brings elation; the ego is easily inflated by skin-tingling religious experiences. In matching the 'super-apostles' Paul speaks of being 'elated' (RSV; *conceited*, NIV) or 'up-lifted' (the Greek word could almost mean 'airborne') by the *surpassingly great revelations* (verse 7). God, however, brought the elated Paul down to

[13] *The Thorn That Remained* (Institute Press, 1972), pp. 8–10.

earth and pinned him there with a 'thorn' (verse 7). Though it was *a messenger of Satan*, the thorn *was given* to Paul – that is, given by God (verse 7).[14] By means of Satan's agency the sovereign God 'gave' Paul what was needful for him. Paul's reference to *a thorn … given* (by God) … , *a messenger of Satan* call to mind the early chapters of the book of Job where the Lord permits Satan to test, but not to kill, Job. God is not the direct but the indirect source of our testing; nevertheless Satan acts within the limits set by God.

Like the Lord in Gethsemane, who prayed more than once, Paul *prayed three times* (verse 8), but to no avail. It was now a matter of submitting to the will of God as he unfolded it. The messengers of Satan are not always overthrown here and now by prevailing prayer, though they will be overthrown ultimately; neither is it necessarily the will of God that his children 'triumph' in this life in terms of body healing or spiritual power. The 'thorn' from God kept Paul from imagining himself as a spiritual superman, and revealed to him the reality of his human mortality and weakness despite his extraordinary revelations. The 'thorn' also kept Paul pinned close to the Lord, in trust and confidence.

c. God's power: perfected in weakness

In response to Paul's thrice-repeated prayer, the Lord answered; and the Greek perfect tense indicates that Paul *still* heard him saying: *My grace is sufficient for you, for my power is made perfect in weakness* (verse 9). Here is the ultimate revelation, which stands for all time. Paul no longer prays for the removal of the 'thorn'. That lies in the past. The 'thorn' is with him still; the Lord's answer rings in his ears still.

The grace of God is not only for the beginning of the Christian life; it is for the beginning, the middle and the end. Through the pain of the 'thorn', Paul was to learn that we get no lasting glory here, least of all through dramatic religious experiences, though they appear glorious and laden with power.

There is a 'power' which brings elation; but it is the power of the flesh, not the power of Christ. It is the newcomers' 'power-in-power', as exemplified in their claim to be 'above' (*hyper*) Paul in missionary travel, ecstasy and revelations. The power of Christ is

[15] A. Schlatter, quoted in F. D. Brunner, *A Theology of the Holy Spirit* (Hodder and Stoughton, 1970), p. 317.

rather power-in-weakness, for his grace is apprehended only in the awareness of our weakness. This is not, we emphasize, merely a warm 'devotional thought'. It is at the very heart of the gospel and the argument of this letter. Paul related how in Asia he had been 'beyond power' (*hyper dynamin*), 'crushed' (1:8). He had acknowledged himself to be an expendable 'jar of clay' who can cope with adversity only by the 'all-surpassing power *of God*' (*hyperbolē ... dynameōs*; 4:7). Paul's ministry, which was marked by such pain, was possible only through the 'power of God' (6:7). The grace and power of God interlock with human lives at the point of mortal weakness. Schlatter wrote that 'the self-centred conception of faith which understands faith as participation of God's power by which one is brought higher life ... a desire to be bound to the exalted Christ without appreciating God's grace in the crucified one, a filling with the Spirit which blesses one with one's own greatness ... all this was in the deepest sense un-Pauline ... and unapostolic'.[15]

There is great glory; but it is not yet. It will be revealed at the end, our afflictions having drawn us closer and closer, throughout our lives, to the grace of Christ. This then, is the climax of Paul's boasting.

In practical terms it means that we accept that we live in God's 'plan B' world and that the ' plan A' world is yet to come. In this present world there are injustice and inequality, and frequently we are helpless to remedy the evil effects of these in our own lives. In this present existence we suffer from disorders within our personalities, and though prayer and counselling may minimize them they are not always removed. In our present lives many suffer from ill-health, mental illness and disease that neither intercession nor medication overcomes. What is the Christian to do in these circumstances of pain and suffering? He is to pray that the Lord will deliver him, as Paul did. It may be that God will deliver the person, as he is continuously doing (1:10; 4:7–10), mindful that all such deliverances are partial. But if not, what then? It is all too easy to allow these things to eat away at our lives until we become embittered and self-pitying. Alternatively, it sometimes happens that suffering Christians turn in desperation to those whose teaching on healing fails to acknowledge that we still live in a 'plan B' world. Rather, the person in Christ is to allow those 'thorns' to pin him

---

[14] Jewish idiom, out of a reverent desire to avoid a direct reference to God, often used a passive verb form to indicate an action performed by God.

closer to Christ who imparts grace to the sufferer both to bear the pain and also to develop qualities of endurance and patience.

In some mysterious way it is within God's plan that our present existence is marked by sin and suffering. From one point of view God abhors and hates these things and will one day overthrow them. And yet is it not through the awareness of our sins that the grace of God holds us near Christ for forgiveness right through our lives? And is it not, also, in the pain of the suffering of both body and mind, that the same grace pins us closer to Christ, who says to us, 'My power is made perfect in weakness'?

d. Ordinary weakness

Paul's letters may be strong but he is, in reality, weak. This is no literary device nor just his opponents' accusation. It is the truth about him; but it is also the truth about the Corinthians. Yet Paul is not boasting of 'special' weakness. It is not weakness induced by religious exercises of fasting or all-night prayer vigils. He has not 'emptied' himself so that he might be 'filled'. It is not a contrived or extraordinary weakness. It is simply the ordinary weakness of a servant of God weary in bone and limb from serving others in the gospel of Christ. 'Just look at me,' he is saying (12:6). 'I am what I appear to be, nothing more. I am open and transparent; I have given you a window into my heart.'

3. It has been for you (12:11–19)

I have made a fool of myself, but you drove me to it. I ought to have been commended by you, for I am not in the least inferior to the 'super-apostles', even though I am nothing. [12]The things that mark an apostle – signs, wonders and miracles – were done among you with great perseverance. [13]How were you inferior to the other churches, except that I was never a burden to you? Forgive me this wrong!

[14]Now I am ready to visit you for the third time, and I will not be a burden to you, because what I want is not your possessions but you. After all, children should not have to save up for their parents, but parents for their children. [15]So I will very gladly spend for you everything I have and expend myself as well. If I love you more, will you love me less? [16]Be that as it may, I have not been a burden to you. Yet, crafty fellow that I am, I caught you by trickery! [17]Did I exploit you through any of the men I sent you? [18]I urged Titus to go to you and I sent our brother with him. Titus did not exploit you, did he? Did we not act in the same spirit and follow the same course?

19Have you been thinking all along that we have been defending ourselves to you? We have been speaking in the sight of God as those in Christ; and everything we do, dear friends, is for your strengthening.

a.   The signs of an apostle

Once again Paul denies any inferiority to *the super-apostles* (verse 11),[16] who appear to have claimed superiority over Paul by virtue of visions and revelations in which they 'heard inexpressible things, things that man is not permitted to tell' (verse 4). Specifically he now points to what is probably a technical phrase, *the things that mark an apostle*, which he amplifies as *signs, wonders and miracles*. The Acts of the Apostles describes some of these – for example the instant healing of the man crippled from birth at Lystra, and the expulsion of the spirit of divination from the slave girl at Philippi.[17]

Such signs provided the visible evidence to those who doubted Paul's claims of God's unique calling of him to be apostle to the Gentiles. Writing to the Jewish and Gentile Christian groups in Rome to prepare them for his coming, Paul mentions his ministry from Jerusalem round to Illyricum (Yugoslavia) accompanied as it was by the power of signs and wonders as evidence that he was, indeed, called by God to be 'a minister ... to the Gentiles'.[18] The phrase *the things that mark an apostle*, then, is not a pointer to numerous 'apostles', loosely defined, who performed miracles. On the contrary, it is a reference to Paul's distinctive and unique calling an an apostle, of which these signs are the visible proof.

That such signs were said to be *done among you* means that it was God who performed them.[19] (It is interesting that the Acts makes no reference to miracles by Paul in Corinth, an indication perhaps of the selective character of Luke's account). His words *with great perseverance* suggest Paul's circumspection in the performance of these signs as opposed to a possibly more spectacular approach adopted by his opponents.

In an era much preoccupied with apostolic signs and wonders, as ours is, we do well to note that not all the apostles' miracles would be welcome in all quarters. Certainly we would appreciate the healing of the chronically crippled man or the raising of the dead Dorcas.[20] But what of the deaths of Ananias and Sapphira or the

---

[16] *Cf.* Rom. 15:18–19.   [17] Acts 14:8–10; 16:16–18.   [18] Rom. 15:16.
[19] See above, footnote 14.   [20] Acts 3:1–10; 9:36–42.

181

temporary blinding of Elymas?[21] These too are signs and wonders!

Moreover, it is vital to distinguish between *the things that mark an apostle*, and spiritual gifts in the churches, which, as I see it, are not limited to the apostles.[22] While we may expect various manifestations of 'extraordinary' as well as 'ordinary' spiritual gifts within the churches, we must insist that apostolic signs and wonders no longer occur, simply because the apostolic age is long past. The very phrase *the things that mark an apostle* clearly implies that only apostles performed them. It should be noted too that Paul nowhere seeks to legitimize his ministry by means of miraculous phenomena. What Paul pointed to as evidence of his genuineness in ministry was faithful evangelism and the resulting existence of congregations of believers (5:11–13; 3:1–3; 10:7).

b. Paul's self-disclosure

The catalogue of boasting, begun in chapter 11, is now ended. Throughout the letter, including these last chapters, Paul has been engaged in a defence of his message and ministry. Now he springs a surprise on the Corinthians. He asks, *Have you been thinking all along that we have been defending ourselves to you?* (verse 19). We would probably reply that what he had written seemed just that – a defence, an apologia for his apostleship. In part, perhaps; yet essentially, it has all been for their sakes.

Paul has written openly about himself and all his weaknesses so that the Corinthians might see in him the reality of their own weaknesses. Their pride has forced Paul to become a weak *fool* before their eyes (verse 11) so that they might identify themselves before God with him. They ought to have commended him because he was a 'true apostle' with *signs, wonders and miracles* to support his claims (verse 12). They should have accepted and respected his leadership. But because they have refused to do so, he has, in love for them, laid himself bare; he has become a *fool* so that they might recognize their own folly.

Not only has he been forced by them to this ignominy; he is also now suspected of coming in order to get their money, or, manipulatively, not to accept their support (verses 14–17). This is too much. Let them understand: he is their father; they are his *children*. He will provide for them; not they for him. To question

---

[21] Acts 5:1–11; 13:6–12.   [22] 1 Cor. 12:4–11.

Paul's integrity in matters relating to money was to add insult to injury.

c. Paul, a pattern to imitate

Thus Paul has made an astonishing disclosure (verse 19). His elaborate statement about being a *fool* which began in 11:1 and which concludes only in 12:10 is not, after all, the self-defence it appears to be – at least, not in its primary intention. Paul, it seems, is engaged in a remarkable exercise in personal communication. It is that he has set himself before them as a pattern. He conveys his teachings with great variety of style. Rather than write abstractly, he has written concretely about himself. The purpose is, clearly, that the Corinthians will *identify* with him and then *imitate* him.

Later he will write very personally to the Philippians (chapter 3), telling them of the acceptance with God he now enjoys in Christ. He will explain his spiritual goals as a man in Christ. Then he will exhort them, 'Join with others in following my example.'[23] In the face of the intruding Judaizing theology, the Philippians were to follow Paul's example in terms of his confidence in Christ and his goal of conformity with Christ,[24] both of which he has given them by his own example.

Earlier he wrote to the Corinthians admonishing them so to adjust their overly high view of freedom out of love for both the weak Christian and the 'not-yet' Christian.[25] But rather than state this teaching abstractly, he set before them at length his own example of personal freedom and rights which are relinquished for the sake of the spiritual needs of others.[26] Then, at the end of the section, he appealed to them, 'Follow my example, as I follow the example of Christ.'[27]

Paul systematically and deliberately lived out the style of a man 'in Christ' so that others might imitate him. He consciously called others to model themselves on the lifestyle which arose out of his own imitation of Christ. Further, both Paul and Peter, when teaching other ministers, called on them to be models for their people to imitate.[28]

It is not merely a question of being a good example so as not to undermine the credibility of what is being taught. It is that Paul

[23] Phil. 3:17; *cf.* 4:9.   [24] Phil. 3:3–4, 14.   [25] 1 Cor. 8.
[26] 1 Cor. 9.   [27] 1 Cor. 11:1.   [28] 1 Tim. 4:12; Tit. 2:7; 1 Pet. 5:3.

183

actively teaches important elements of Christian thought and behaviour by means of his manner of life which he deliberately sets before others. The self-disclosure in 11:1 – 12:10 that he is *weak* and a *fool* is another example of this method of teaching Christian truth and behaviour.

4. The final visit: test yourselves (12:20 – 13:4)

For I am afraid that when I come I may not find you as I want you to be, and you may not find me as you want me to be. I fear that there may be quarrelling, jealousy, outbursts of anger, factions, slander, gossip, arrogance and disorder. 21I am afraid that when I come again my God will humble me before you, and I will be grieved over many who have sinned earlier and have not repented of the impurity, sexual sin and debauchery in which they have indulged.

13:1This will be my third visit to you. 'Every matter must be established by the testimony of two or three witnesses.' 2I already gave you a warning when I was with you the second time. I now repeat it while absent: On my return I will not spare those who sinned earlier or any of the others, 3since you are demanding proof that Christ is speaking through me. He is not weak in dealing with you, but is powerful among you. 4For to be sure, he was crucified in weakness, yet he lives by God's power. Likewise, we are weak in him, yet by God's power we will live with him to serve you.

a. Moral deterioration in Corinth (12: 20–21)

Paul's final visit to Corinth is now imminent. This part of the letter is obviously preparing the way for what will almost certainly be a tense arrival. Twice the apostle expresses fear. He is *afraid* that, because they will not be as he wants them to be nor he what they want him to be, there will be *quarrelling, jealousy, outbursts of anger, factions, slander, gossip, arrogance and disorder* (verse 20). Paul, it seems, anticipates that the third visit, like the second, would prove to be painful. He also fears that because *many* continue unrepentant of gross sexual offences he will be grieved for them (verse 21). This serious situation he had observed and learned about on his second visit (13:2).

In writing his first letter Paul drew attention to the dramatic moral conversion which some of the Corinthians had undergone.[29] There were others, however, who believed that everything was permissible, including fornication.[30] Despite the 'painful' visit and

[29] 1 Cor. 6:9–11.   [30] 1 Cor. 6:12–20.

the 'sorrowful' letter, this libertine attitude had persisted; and Paul is, it seems, apprehensive about dealing with the matter once again (verse 21).

We may infer that the arrival of the newcomers had hindered rather than helped in the moral problems of the Corinthians. His reference to the weak Christians being led into sin (11:29) is in the general context of the newcomers' ministry in Corinth (11:13–15, 20). Despite the Judaizers' supposed emphasis on the Jewish law and morality, they actually led the Corinthians away from their 'sincere and pure devotion to Christ' (11:3) and therefore away from the life-changing power of the Holy Spirit.[31]

b. Power in weakness (13:1–4)

Paul refers to his projected visit to Corinth in what is to us a very puzzling manner. What does he mean by *every matter*, *testimony*, *witnesses* (verse 1)? This sounds like some kind of a court hearing. The reference to grief (12:21) appears to echo the grief which seems to have occurred after the 'court hearing' described in the first letter.[32] In our reconstruction,[33] a charge was first made which had to *be established by the testimony of two or three witnesses* (verse 1).[34] A judgment would then be made, the apostle being present either 'physically' or 'in spirit',[35] and, if the accused were guilty, Paul would not *spare* him (verse 2). It is not clear whether the offender was then removed, or whether the congregation withdrew its fellowship from the offender.[36] The unrepentant offender now being 'handed over to Satan',[37] that is, reckoned as under judgment, he became the object of 'grief'. What kind of sin warrants this severe treatment? The evidence from both letters suggests gross sexual offences. In the first letter it is apparently a case of incest.[38] In this letter Paul refers to 'impurity, sexual sin and debauchery' (12:21) which were 'not repented of', that is, they were still being practised.

Paul had apparently observed this on his *second* (or 'painful') visit and warned that on his return he would *not spare* the offenders (verse 2), by which, in our reconstruction, he meant the holding of the quasi-judicial hearing followed by the grief for the unrepentant.

---

[31] 1 Cor. 6:11; 2 Cor. 3:18.
[32] 1 Cor. 5:2–5.
[33] Was this court based on synagogue hearings (Mk. 13:9)?
[34] *Cf.* Dt. 19:15.   [35] 1 Cor. 5:3.   [36] 1 Cor. 5:2, 11–13.
[37] 1 Cor. 5:5.   [38] 1 Cor. 5:1.

The newcomers have disparaged Paul as weak, claiming that *Christ* was *not speaking through* him (verse 3; *cf.* 10:7). Paul, however, will come in the spiritual and moral power of the living Christ. Christ indeed was weak in his death, as Paul is in his life (verse 4), a fact which he has been acknowledging (12:9). But Christ *lives by God's power* and is powerful in dealing with the Corinthians (verses 3–4). Paul, too, will be powerful in dealing with them since he *will live with* Christ *by God's power* (verse 4). Paul will not come in the supposed power of visions or ecstasy but in the power of a godly man 'in Christ', who will exhort, judge and grieve over the unrepentant. Like the Corinthian church at that time, many churches today, and church people, are subject to great moral temptation, to which they sometimes succumb. Like Paul, we must be prepared to exhort, encourage, and discipline those who have fallen into sin as well as restore the penitent.

5. Test yourselves (13:5–13)

Examine yourselves to see whether you are in the faith; test yourselves. Do you not realise that Christ Jesus is in you – unless, of course, you fail the test? [6]*And I trust that you will discover that we have not failed the test.* [7]*Now we pray to God that you will not do anything wrong. Not that people will see that we have stood the test but that you will do what is right even though we may seem to have failed.* [8]*For we cannot do anything against the truth, but only for the truth.* [9]*We are glad whenever we are weak but you are strong; and our prayer is for your perfection.* [10]*This is why I write these things when I am absent, that when I come I may not have to be harsh in my use of authority – the authority the Lord gave me for building you up, not for tearing you down.*
    [11]*Finally, brothers, good-bye. Aim for perfection, listen to my appeal, be of one mind, live in peace. And the God of love and peace will be with you.*
    [12]*Greet one another with a holy kiss.* [13]*All the saints send their greetings.*

Having made his warnings (verse 2), Paul now concludes his letter on a positive and optimistic note. Rather than seek *proof* that Christ speaks through Paul (verse 3), let the Corinthians be reminded that in fact *Jesus Christ is in* them (verse 5). The *proof* of Paul's ministry to the Corinthians is related to the 'proof' that they are in fact Christian. Thus Paul (verse 6) expects them to discover that he has *not failed*.[40] While this is not unimportant to Paul, what he prays is

[39] In Greek, this verb (*dokimazein*) is related to the word for 'proof' (*dokimē*).
[40] That is, been 'dis-proved' (*adokimoi*).

186

that the Corinthians may *not do anything wrong* but that they may *do what is right* (verse 7). Let them repent of these gross sins (12:21) and also see the newcomers in a true light.

Our prayer, he tells them in verse 9, *is for your perfection*, or, better, their 'mending'.[41] Paul's primary concern was their 'mending' as a Christian community. What will encourage Paul is the knowledge that the Corinthians are *strong* Christians (verse 9). The *authority* which *the Lord gave* Paul as apostle was for the *building up* of Christians and churches (verse 10), not *tearing down* (by which he apparently means the necessary but negative process of judging and mourning; 12:21 – 13:2). Therefore, in the period before he comes, let them *aim for perfection, listen to* his *appeal, be of one mind*, and *live in peace* (verse 11). As he prayed for their 'mending', so now he exhorts them to 'mend your ways' (verse 11, RSV), or, literally, to 'be mended'. God answers our prayers as we actively pursue his will. In the pastoral appeal which follows, Paul exhorts them to *listen to* his *appeal*, to *be of one mind*, to live in peace and to *greet one another with a holy kiss*. In their obedience to this the *God of love and peace will be with* them (verse 11), and the 'mending' for which he has prayed will become a reality.

We are curious to know what the Corinthians did in response to Paul's letter. Did they continue as they were, allowing the newcomers to exert their influence? Or did they heed the apostle? The fact that the letter was not torn up when the Corinthians received it and that it has come down to us suggests that they deferred to Paul. When Paul arrived in Corinth, he stayed three months[42] and wrote the letter to the Romans, where there are only faint echoes of the present difficulties. We conclude that the Corinthians and the apostle were reconciled.

6. Final prayer (13:14)

May the grace of the Lord Jesus Christ, and the love of God, and the fellowship of the Holy Spirit be with you all.

Paul concludes his letter with the beautiful prayer whose very familiarity has perhaps caused us to miss the point he is making. The three persons of the Trinity are mentioned, but in the order which reflects Christian experience. First, there is *the grace of the Lord*

---

[41] The verb is that used of James and John when they were 'mending' their nets (Mk. 1:19, RSV).   [42] Acts 20:2–3.

Jesus Christ which is encountered in the 'message of reconciliation' (5:19; 6:1) and through which we are made 'rich' (8:9). Then, as a consequence, we come to know the *love of God* from the one Paul has just described as 'the God of love' (verse 11). Finally, also as a consequence, we experience *the fellowship of the Holy Spirit*, which refers to the Spirit's fellowship with our spirits[43] and also the fellowship which exists between those in whom the Spirit of God dwells.[44]

By this prayer Paul is reminding the Corinthians that their 'mending' does not lie within themselves but with the grace of Christ, the love of God and the Spirit's fellowship. The grace of Christ removes aggressiveness, the love of God dispels jealousy, while the fellowship created by the Spirit destroys bitterness. As God answers that prayer, the problems so manifest in Corinth and in every troubled church will be overcome.

[43] *Cf.* Rom. 8:16.   [44] 1 Cor. 3:16.